Medical Law in Switzerland

Medical Law in Switzerland

Second Edition

Andrea Büchler & Thomas Gächter

This book was originally published as a monograph in the International Encyclopaedia of Laws/Medical Law.

General Editors: Roger Blanpain, Frank Hendrickx
Volume Editor: Herman Nys

Stämpfli Publishers

Wolters Kluwer

Published by:
Kluwer Law International B.V.
PO Box 316
2400 AH Alphen aan den Rijn
The Netherlands
Website: www.wklawbusiness.com

Sold and distributed in North, Central and South America by:
Wolters Kluwer Legal & Regulatory U.S.
7201 McKinney Circle
Frederick, MD 21704
United States of America
Email: customer.service@wolterskluwer.com

Sold and Distributed in Switzerland by:
Stämpfli Publishers Ltd.
Wölflistr. 1, P.O. Box 5662
CH-3001 Berne
Switzerland
E-mail: verlag@staempfli.com
Phone: +41 31 300 66 44
Website: www.staempfliverlag.com

Sold and distributed in all other countries by:
Turpin Distribution Services Ltd.
Stratton Business Park
Pegasus Drive, Biggleswade
Bedfordshire SG18 8TQ
United Kingdom
Email: kluwerlaw@turpin-distribution.com

ISBN 978-90-411-8265-4 (Kluwer)
ISBN 978-3-7272-7772-6 (Stämpfli)

This title is available on www.kluwerlawonline.com

The Authors

Prof. Dr iur. Andrea Büchler joined the University of Zurich as Professor of Law in 2002. She holds the chair of private and comparative law. Her areas of research are family law, law of persons, comparative law, Islamic and Middle Eastern law, medicine and law, and legal gender studies. She founded the Centre for Islamic and Middle Eastern Legal Studies at the Faculty of Law of the University of Zurich in 2008. In 2003, she co-founded the Centre for Family Sciences, a Switzerland-wide association that initiates, conducts, and supports high-quality research in the field of the family. She has been the co-leader of the training as a specialist solicitor in family law since 2007. She was awarded a fellowship at the Institute of Advanced Studies, Berlin, for the academic year 2008/2009 and a fellowship at The Straus Institute for the Advanced Study in Law and Social Justice at NYU, New York, for the academic year 2011/2012. She was a Visiting Professor at the University of California Berkeley, Boalt Hall School of Law, and she is a Fellow at the Collegium Helveticum ETH/UZH.

Andrea Büchler earned her MA, PhD, and venia docendi in Private Law, Comparative Law, and Gender Law between 1990 and 2002 at the University of Basle, Switzerland. Her recent activities include leadership of the interdisciplinary and interinstitutional research project 'Children and Divorce – Current Legal Practices and Their Impact on Family Transitions' and the project 'Legal Gender Studies – a Commented List of Sources', both financed by the Swiss National Science Foundation (SNF), as well as research focused on legal pluralism in Europe and the publication of an extensive comment on the Swiss federal law on registered partnerships and on medical law. She is a member of a number of legal research networks and institutions both within and outside universities. Since 2016, she is the President of the National Advisory Committee of Biomedical Ethics, NEK.

The Authors

Prof. Dr iur. Thomas Gächter holds the chair of constitutional law, administrative law, and social security law at the Faculty of Law of the University of Zurich (since 2006). He is at the same time a visiting professor for social security law and health law at the University of Lucerne. After university education at the universities of Zurich and Louvain (Belgium), he graduated in Zurich and worked as a scientific assistant at the Chair of Prof. Dr Alfred Koelz (University of Zurich). In his practical work, he was a clerk of the justice at the Court of Administrative Law in Zurich. In 2002, he obtained a doctoral degree at the University of Zurich and was in the same year appointed as a lecturer ('*Privatdozent*') at the same university. From 2004 to 2006, he was an associate professor at the University of Lucerne (social security law) and research professor of the Swiss National Fund with a project on the fundaments of Swiss social security law at the University of Zurich. He teaches constitutional law, administrative law, social security law, and health law. He is the author of a standard textbook in health law, as well as other publications in this field. He works on different projects in health law, social security law, and constitutional law.

Table of Contents

Table of Contents

List of Abbreviations

BGE	Ruling of the Swiss Federal Supreme Court
BV	Federal Constitution of the Swiss Confederation of 18 April 1999 (*Bundesverfassung*, SR 101)
cf.	Confer (compare, consult)
ClinO	Ordinance on Clinical Trials in Human Research (Clinical Trials Ordinance; ClinO; *Verordnung vom 20. September 2013 über klinische Versuche in der Humanforschung [Verordnung über klinische Versuche*; *KlinV], SR 810.305*)
CRUS	Rector's Conference of Swiss Universities
De lege lata	*Nach geltendem Recht*, the law as it exists
DSG	Data Privacy Law (*Bundesgesetz vom 19. Juni 1992 über den Datenschutz, SR 235.1*)
EC	European Community
ECHR	European Court of Human Rights / European Convention on Human Rights
ed.	Edition
Eds	Editors
EEA	European Economic Area
EFTA	European Free Trade Association
e.g.	*Exempli gratia* (for example)
ECHR	European Convention on Human Rights
EJPD	Federal Department of Justice and Police
EOG	*Erwerbsersatzordnung*, Income Replacement Regulation
Epidemic Law	*Bundesgesetz vom 18. Dezember 1970 über die Bekämpfung übertragbarer Krankheiten des Menschen, SR 818.101*
etc.	*Et cetera*
et seq.	*Et sequens*
EU	European Union

List of Abbreviations

EU-27	European Union, twenty-seven Member States
EXIT	Assisted Dying Organization in Switzerland
FADP	Federal Act of 19 June 1992 on Data Protection
FamPra	Practice in Family Law
ff.	And the following
FMedG	Federal Act on Medically Assisted Reproduction (Reproductive Medicine Act), (*Bundesgesetz über die medizinisch unterstützte Fortpflanzung vom 18. Dezember 1998, SR 810.11*)
FMH	Swiss Medical Association
GDP	Gross Domestic Product
GUMG	Federal Law on Genetic Tests on Humans (*Bundesgesetz vom 8. Oktober 2004 über genetische Untersuchungen beim Menschen, SR 810.12*)
HFG	Law on Research on Human Beings (*Bundesgesetz über die Forschung am Menschen vom 30. September 2011, Humanforschungsgesetz, SR 810.30*)
HMG	Federal Act on Medicinal Products and Medical Devices (*Therapeutic Products Act*), (*Bundesgesetz vom 15. Oktober 2000 über Arzneimittel und Medizinprodukte, SR 812.21*)
HMO	Health Maintenance Organization
HRO	Ordinance on Human Research with the Exception of Clinical Trials (Human Research Ordinance, HRO; *Verordnung vom 20. September 2013 über die Humanforschung mit Ausnahme der klinischen Versuche [Humanforschungsverordnung, HFV]*, SR 810.301)
i.e.	*Id est*
ILO	International Labour Organization
IVG	Disability Insurance Law (*Bundesgesetz vom 19. Juni 1959 über die Invalidenversicherung, SR 831.20*)
KLV	Health Insurance Service Ordinance (*Krankenpflege-Leistungsverordnung*)
KVG	Health Insurance Law (*Bundesgesetz vom 18. März 1994 über die Krankenversicherung, SR 832.10*)
KVV	Health Insurance Ordinance (*Verordnung vom 27. Juni 1995 über die Krankenversicherung, SR 832.102*)
Lex specialis	Special Law
MedBG	Federal Law of the Medical Professions
Ne bis in idem	Not twice for the same

NEK	National Ethics Commission for Human Medicine
No.	*Numero*, number
Nr.	Number
OECD	Organisation for Economic Co-operation and Development
OR	Swiss Code of Obligations (*Bundesgesetz vom 30. März 1911 betreffend die Ergänzung des Schweizerischen Zivilgesetzbuches, fünfter Teil: Obligationenrecht, SR 220*)
OrgO-HRL	Ordinance on Organisational Aspects of the Law on Research on Human Beings (HRL Organisation Ordinance, OrgO-HRL; *Organisationsverordnung vom 20. September 2013 zum Humanforschungsgesetz [Organisationsverordnung HFG, OV-HFG]*, SR 810.308)
Per se	In itself, itself
SAMW	Swiss Academy of the Medical Sciences
SIWF	Swiss Institute for Postgraduate and Continuing Medical Education
SR	Classified Compilation of the Federal Legislation
StaO FMH	Code of the Professional Conduct of the FMH (*Standesordnung der FMH*)
Sterilisation Law	Swiss Code of Sterilisation (*Bundesgesetz über Voraussetzungen und Verfahren bei Sterilisationen vom 17. Dezember 2004, SR 211.111.1*)
StFG	Stem Cell Research Law (*Bundesgesetz vom 19. Dezember 2003 über die Forschung an embryonalen Stammzellen, SR 810.31*)
StGB	Swiss Penal Code (*Schweizerisches Strafgesetzbuch vom 21. Dezember 1937, SR 311.0*)
TARMED	Tarif Medical
Transplantation Law	Federal Act of 8 October 2004 on the Transplantation of Tissues Organs, and Cells (*Bundesgesetz über die Transplantation von Organen, Geweben und Zellen, SR 810.21*)
UN	United Nations
UN Covenant I	United Nations Covenant I
UN Covenant II	United Nations Covenant II
UN Disabilities Convention	United Nations Convention on the Rights of Persons with Disabilities
VLSS	Association of Chief Hospital Doctors
Vol.	Volume

List of Abbreviations

VSAO	Association of Swiss Assistant and Senior Physicians
ZEK	Central Ethics Commission
ZGB	Swiss Civil Code (*Schweizerisches Zivilgesetzbuch vom 10. Dezember 1907, SR 210*)

General Introduction

§1. General Background of the Country

I. Geography

1. Switzerland is a landlocked country in the heart of Western Europe, surrounded by Germany, Austria, Liechtenstein, Italy, and France. It has a surface area of 41,285 square kilometres and its border measures 1,858 kilometres in circumference. Switzerland is divided into 26 cantons and 2,352 municipalities.

2. The country has 8,237,666 inhabitants, with an average of 203.5 inhabitants per square kilometre. In comparison to other European countries, Switzerland is very densely populated.

3. The population is concentrated largely in the urban regions in the midlands between Lake Geneva and Lake Constance. The more rural areas and peripheral regions are less populated. Switzerland's highest population density is centred in five large cities. Zurich, the country's largest city, has 391,400 inhabitants, Geneva 194,600, Basel 168,600, Bern 130,000, and Lausanne 133,900.

4. The climate in the north of Switzerland varies greatly from the south. Because of the Alps, which act as a prominent climate barrier running east to west, Switzerland's northern regions are distinguished by a moderate central European climate often affected by Atlantic winds, whereas the southern part enjoys Mediterranean summers and milder winters.

II. Cultural Composition

5. Switzerland's population is not united by a single language. Traditionally, the four languages of the country are German, French, Italian, and Romansh.

6. German is spoken by 63.5% of the population, primarily in north-eastern and central Switzerland as well as in parts of Valais Canton. French-speaking Swiss make up 22.5% of the population, and they live in the western part of the country. In Tessin and in certain regions of Grisons, Italian (8.1%) and – only in Grisons – Romansh (0.5%) are spoken.

7. The various population groups living in Switzerland are marked by great diversity. At the end of 2014, 1,998,459 foreign nationals were living in the country. The foreign portion of the permanent resident population is comparatively high at 24.3%. Only Liechtenstein and Luxembourg have higher percentages in Europe.

8. A total of 85% of the foreign resident population comes from Europe. Two-thirds of foreigners (66.4%) hail from one of the twenty-eight European Union countries (EU-28) or from countries with membership in the European Free Trade Association (EFTA).

9. Just as the people of Switzerland are heterogeneous with respect to their language and ancestry, so too are they diverse in terms of religion and denominations. In various cantons, there are three established regional churches – the Roman Catholic Church (38.2%), Christ Catholic Church (0.15%), and Evangelical Reformed Church (26.9%). The largest religious minorities consist of Muslims (5%) and Jews (0.3%), while 21.4% of the population has no religious affiliation. The remaining portion of the population belongs to another Christian community or religious association.

III. Political System

A. Federalism

10. Switzerland consists of a total of twenty-six federal states (cantons) that differ widely in terms of their respective sizes and populations. The canton with the smallest population, Appenzell Innerrhoden, has only 15,854 inhabitants; the canton with the largest population, Zurich, has roughly 1.5 million. The canton with the smallest surface area is Basel-City, with about 37 square kilometres, and the largest is Grisons, covering some 7,106 square kilometres.

11. Basically, all cantons enjoy equal rights. Only six of the cantons have half of a canton-vote in Swiss plebiscites in which a federalist majority is required. These cantons are also only allowed to elect one – as opposed to two – members to the Council of States (the second house of parliament).

12. The cantons are historically evolved polities that have pronounced autonomy in terms of lawmaking, enforcement, and organization.

13. The Swiss healthcare system can only be understood against the backdrop of this distinctly federalist fragmentation of the country. Numerous core areas of health law – e.g., the upkeep of inpatient medical infrastructures – come within cantonal purview. As a result, the cantons have very different regulations in important areas.

B. Governmental System

1. Key Features of the Swiss Governmental System at a Federal Level

14. The following key features of the Swiss political system are important to understanding some characteristics of Swiss legislation:

- The government is elected by parliament for a fixed term; the government may not be voted out of office preterm.
- The government may not dissolve parliament.
- There is collective government: decisions are made by a body whose members have equal rights.
- There is no head of state; the Federal President is merely the '*primus inter pares*' in the government.
- There is multi-party government (the concordance system).
- The people can assume an oppositional role by dint of their direct democratic rights.

2. Significance of Direct Democracy

15. The Swiss political system is strongly characterized by the people's direct democratic rights of participation. The people have extensive rights of participation at all levels of government. At the Federal level, there is the optional referendum on laws, the compulsory constitutional referendum, the referendum on international treaties, and the constitutional initiative. There is a possibility of initiating laws almost everywhere at the cantonal level. Moreover, cantonal governments are directly elected by the people.

16. The optional referendum on laws, existing since 1874, has had a special influence on the political system. The system is generally designated as concordance democracy, consensual democracy, or referendum democracy. Common to all three of these terms is the stress they place on the importance of consensus and compromise for the Swiss style of government. In contrast to the parliamentary system, this is a political system in which governmental power is apportioned among the most important political currents, and parliament and government are controlled by the people through special referendums. The opposition role is thus assumed by the people together with individual parties. The system presupposes a certain stability and, above all, the presence of political determination to take collective action.

17. As a consequence of these highly developed referendum rights, the government and legislature are forced to draft bills with majority appeal so that they can survive any possible referendum. The result is that the legislative process becomes a search for a political compromise that can eventually withstand a referendum. This in turn strengthens the importance of the 'legislative process by consultation', by which interested groups can participate in the Federal government's shaping of opinion and in the decision-making process. Corresponding political positions carry great weight, particularly when the participants in the legislative process by consultation (especially cantons, political parties, and pressure groups) are so big and financially powerful that they are in a position to mount a referendum campaign.

18. And it is particularly in health policy, which is dominated by various pressure groups, that the possibility of a referendum plays a decisive role in the political opinion-making process.

19. The constant 'threat of intervention' by a referendum weakens the political system's ability to renew itself. By contrast, the popular initiative frequently functions as an agent of innovation, as an engine of the political system. But this happens less by way of direct acceptance of such initiatives through the people than through their indirect impact, as officials and parties are forced to develop direct or indirect counterproposals to the reform initiatives, which then often find majorities in national referendums.

20. In recent years, there have been several popular initiatives launched in the area of health that have given new impetus to the system. But only two counterproposals to a constitutional initiative were accepted: one demanding greater consideration of complementary medicine in healthcare (Article 118a, BV), the other strengthening primary healthcare and the role of the family doctors in the healthcare system (Article 117a, BV).

3. Parliament and Government

21. The Swiss Federal Constitution of 1874 as well as its successor of 1999 both stress the democratic principle by providing for the people's aforementioned direct rights of participation and by placing the parliament above a government only indirectly legitimized by the national elections. Furthermore, the constitution establishes a relatively weak judiciary in comparison with other countries such as Germany.

22. The parliament, the Federal Assembly, consists of two chambers. The National Council is the 'People's Parliament' and is composed of 200 members. The individual cantons form the electoral districts, and the number of seats is proportional to their population. In the National Council, every canton obtains at least one seat. The second chamber is the Council of States and has forty-six members. It is on an equal legal footing with the National Council in all essential matters. Every canton elects two members to the Council of States, but the six cantons possessing only half of a vote have merely a single seat in the chamber. Through its essentially equal distribution of seats, the Council of States strongly underscores the Swiss state's federalist element.

23. The government consists of seven ministers who are each elected by the united Federal Assembly for a period of four years and who constitute a council whose members are placed on an equal footing. Until the succeeding ministerial elections, parliament has no political means of forcing the council or one of the government ministers to resign. The ministers, who are usually chosen from the parliamentary ranks, must forfeit their seat in parliament following their election. But the separation between the executive and legislative branches of government is not as strict as in countries such as the United States, since the ministers can personally champion their bills in parliament and in the various commissions with great effectiveness.

24. Now and in the past, this 'referendum democracy' has been the main reason that Switzerland's four largest parties – the Liberal Democrats, the Christian Democratic People's Party, the Social Democrats, and the Swiss People's Party – are compelled to jointly participate in the government. Otherwise one of them could cripple the system by all too frequently calling for referendums. But despite the cooperation of the largest parties in the Federal Assembly, one cannot really speak of a 'grand coalition', since that common feature of parliamentary governmental systems – parliamentarians voting along their party line – is not a highly developed practice in Switzerland. This is not only a result of the four-year term to which the government is elected but also a consequence of the traditionally weak position of Swiss political parties, particularly at the Federal level. In the Council of States, whose members are chosen by the majority voting system (excepting those from the canton of Jura), the parliamentarians' toe the party line less often than in the National Council, where a proportional voting system is in effect.

C. Relationship with the European Union

25. Switzerland is not a member of the European Union (EU). The slim majority that decided to reject Switzerland's entrance into the European Economic Area (EEA) in 1992 led to an enduring political paralysis of Switzerland's European policy. Switzerland's relationship with the European Union is essentially regulated by a series of bilateral treaties that have partially integrated Switzerland into the European market. Accession to the European Union is presently not on the political agenda.

26. Of particular importance is Switzerland's agreement with the European Union and its Member States on the free movement of persons, which has been in effect since 2002. This agreement guarantees citizens of an EU Member State free access to the Swiss job market and Swiss citizens unrestricted access to the European job market. It also encompasses the medical professions and allows qualified EU physicians to practise in Switzerland. The agreement on free movement of persons is at risk, because on 9 February 2014, the Swiss people and the cantons voted in favour to limit immigration by introducing a yearly maximum number of immigrants and contingents in relation to the overall economic interest. The European Union considers contingents and maximum numbers as a violation of the agreement. At the moment, negotiations are taking place between Switzerland and the European Union to find a settlement. It is unsure if the agreement will be recalled.

IV. Population and Vital Statistics

27. Of Switzerland's 8,237,666 inhabitants, 17.8% are over 64 years old and thus number among the country's oldest population segment. A total of 20.2% of the population consists of children and youth up to 19 years of age. Persons of employable age (from 20 to 64) constitute the largest population group. The age distribution of Switzerland's population has changed considerably over the course of the twentieth century. The baby boomers born between 1959 and 1971 now dominate, while the younger generation occupies a much weaker position and the number of older people has grown over the past few years.

28. The reason for the change in age distribution is not only the decrease in the percentage of children and young people in the total population but, above all, higher life expectancy. Whereas the life expectancy of a male child born in Switzerland in 2001 was 77.4, it increased to 81.0 in 2014. The situation for women is similar: in 2001, the life expectancy for a female child was 83.1 years, and in 2014 it stood at 85.2 years. Swiss life expectancy is very high in comparison with the rest of the world.

29. As result of the increasing numbers of older people in Switzerland, the common causes of death have changed. Diseases of aging are more numerous and are more often the reason for a person's death. Various cancer-related diseases are becoming ever more frequent.

30. The following table presents the numbers of deaths per 100,000 inhabitants and the important causes of death as divided along gender lines (2013):

Causes of Death	*Deaths 2013*		*Mortality Rate 2013*	
	Men	*Women*	*Men*	*Women*
All causes of death	31,275	33,704	555.0	371.0
Infectious diseases	352	415	6.4	4.8
Total cases of cancer	9,200	7,475	167.0	107.0
Large intestine, cancer of	584	583	10.3	7.4
Lungs, cancer of	1,960	1,208	36.5	19.4
Breast, cancer of	5	1,329	0.1	20.0
Diabetes mellitus	615	700	10.6	6.8
Dementia	1,797	4,110	28.5	34.5
Circulatory system	9,719	11,793	164.0	109.0
Total cases of heart disease	7,663	8,984	130.0	81.3
Ischemic heart disease	4,097	3,628	69.9	33.4
Diseases of the cerebral vessels	1,465	2,238	24.3	21.5

Causes of Death	*Deaths 2013*		*Mortality Rate 2013*	
	Men	*Women*	*Men*	*Women*
Total number of diseases of the respiratory system	2,167	1,949	36.4	20.4
Alcoholic cirrhosis of the liver	319	121	6.5	2.3
Accidents and trauma	2,177	1,642	44.0	21.0
Accidents	1,312	1,285	25.3	13.7
Suicide	786	284	16.9	6.0

Source: 'Todesursachenstatistik', Bundesamt für Statistik.

31. Population growth today is around 1.2%. This population growth has little to do with the recent rise in births (live births 2014: 85,287), since women of child-bearing age have an average of only 1.54 children in Switzerland. The constantly sinking infant mortality rate (4.3) is also not a determining factor. The main reason is the gains from immigration. Since 1986, the number of foreign nationals immigrating to Switzerland has exceeded the number of Swiss leaving.

V. Social and Cultural Values

A. *In General*

32. Switzerland's great cultural diversity is the result of centuries of linguistic and religious pluralism.

33. The common elements are a quite liberal attitude, also among parties of the left, as well as an open-mindedness that expressly endorses direct democracy. But such attitudes have not always been apparent in the polarizing political conflicts of the last years – conflicts that have been dominated by xenophobic and nationalistic tendencies. However, the aforementioned values continue to find expression in legislation and in the majority of national referendums.

B. *Basic Attitudes in the Sphere of Healthcare*

34. The entire Swiss population enjoys a high standard of healthcare, and pro-capita healthcare expenditures are exceedingly high. Starting in 1999, Switzerland joined the United States and France as countries with the highest expenditures. Healthcare costs constitute about 11% of the Gross Domestic Product (GPD). By contrast, the costs for disease prevention and health promotion are low, constituting only 2.2% of total healthcare expenditures.

35. Even if Switzerland has recently been the target of international criticism because its immunization rate for measles is considered too low to prevent epidemics, the Organisation for Economic Co-operation and Development (OECD) ranks Switzerland among the countries with the highest immunization rates.

36. Swiss citizens are used to paying part of their healthcare costs themselves. For example, with the exceptions of accidents involving people with accident insurance, the costs of dentistry are usually not covered by social insurance. Moreover, through cost-sharing (above all, a deductible called a 'franchise'), all insured persons assume a defined level of costs for the services covered by compulsory health insurance.

37. Health policy is a very divisive issue in Switzerland. The rising costs – and the growing burden to households due to health insurance premiums whose rates are set independent of household income – are leading to ever more frequent healthcare policy initiatives by government and parliament and to a growing number of popular initiatives. In all these referendums, it is clearly the case that the people place great value on high-quality healthcare to which the entire population has guaranteed access. Thus far, all attempts to appreciably curtail the scope of services provided by obligatory healthcare have failed.

38. Furthermore, in summer 2009 it became clear that people desired that greater account be taken of complementary medicine in healthcare policy. Thus, in that same year, a corresponding bill was passed with a large majority. Up until now, the healthcare system and health insurance have been based on conventional medicine. Moreover, in 2014 people accepted a counterproposal to a constitutional initiative, which was aimed at strengthening primary healthcare and the role of the family doctors.

§2. General Description of the Healthcare System

I. General Review of the Healthcare System

39. Switzerland has a highly developed healthcare system. Seen from an international perspective, capacities in the outpatient sphere are extremely high and inpatient capacities are clearly above the OECD average.

40. The determining factor in Swiss healthcare is the national health insurance system, which also pays for treatment in the case of accidents that are not covered by accident insurance. Because Swiss health insurance is set up as a kind of 'people's' insurance for all inhabitants of the country, the level of services provided by the health insurance determines the standard for all of Switzerland.

41. Basically, there are two areas where costs are not assumed by health insurance: dental treatment and psychotherapy if it is not prescribed or provided by a physician.

42. Like all healthcare systems, the Swiss system is struggling with a massive rise in costs. Because the health insurance premiums are raised every year as per-capita premiums, the insured are made to feel the growing volume of health insurance costs.

43. From a legal standpoint, the Swiss health system is distinguished by a pronounced fragmentation. In important areas such as hospital care, the regulatory levels are not uniform. Whereas the cantons and frequently the municipalities are responsible for operating and guaranteeing inpatient care, at the Federal level, health insurance laws define which costs within the inpatient institutions are assumed by the insurance and on what scale they are to be covered.

44. From a structural point of view, the Swiss healthcare system is very decentralized. Although plans for restructuring hospitals along uniform lines have been in the works since 1996, parallel hospital structures are still frequently maintained in close proximity to one another. One of the reasons is that hospital planning is in the hands of the cantons, which often cannot or will not close their own hospitals due to political considerations. Nevertheless, parts of the cost intensive highly specialized medicine have been coordinated by an agreement between all cantons.

45. Physicians in private practice are the most important contact point for initial treatment in rural and semi-rural areas, whereas in urban areas one can discern a certain tendency to use the outpatient sections of hospitals for initial treatment. The new Article 117a, BV takes the importance of the family doctors in account now.

46. Due to a variety of factors, an increasing number of medical practices are being set up as group practices with shared resources or even as public limited companies. In such establishments doctors are increasingly working as employees, which until recently was the exception in the sphere of private practice.

II. Regulation of the Healthcare System

A. Structure of the Healthcare System

47. There are historical reasons for the lack of basic norms on healthcare at all regulatory levels (municipal, cantonal, Federal, or international). As late as the nineteenth century, protecting the population's health was traditionally a local or, at most, regional responsibility (hygiene regulations, health supervisory authorities, etc.). To the extent that it was necessary, this was shifted to ever higher regulatory levels as social mobility increased and the economy grew more interconnected. In certain cases, only international norms can guarantee adequate health protection. Moreover, the rise of health and accident insurance as economic safeguards against threats to health led to the regulation of these matters at a higher (Federal) level through state bodies (marking a shift away from voluntary self-help organizations).

48. In the division of powers in the Swiss system, the Federal government is only responsible for the regulation of a certain question if the Swiss Federal Constitution ascribes it the authority to do so (Article 3 and Article 42, BV). Basically, as an expression of the Federal principle of subsidiarity, only those responsibilities requiring uniform regulation at the Federal level may be assumed by the Federal government (see Articles 43a and 5a of the BV).

B. Federal Powers

49. Article 117, paragraph 1, of the Swiss Federal Constitution likely constitutes the most important jurisdictional norm at the Federal level. In cursory language and without going into details, this provision stipulates that the Federal government is required to enact regulations concerning health and accident insurance. In both of these spheres, the Federal government has wide-ranging authority, which it has fully exploited by enacting the Federal Health Insurance Law and the Federal Accident Insurance Law. It must be noted, however, that certain cantonal regulatory provisos (e.g., reduction of premiums) are contained in the *Bundesgesetz über die Krankenversicherung* (KVG), or Health Insurance Law.

50. Health insurance and accident insurance are the two systems of reimbursement that fund some 43% of all health costs (or curative costs). Therefore, the laws governing fees and payments in both branches of insurance have considerable repercussions on the range of services and their quality. Thus, healthcare policy at the Federal level is frequently only understood as health insurance policy – which does not do justice to actual circumstances.

51. Some may find it astonishing that Article 95, paragraph 1, of the Swiss Federal Constitution – which succinctly states that the Federal government can enact provisions regarding employment in the private sector – is considered part of the constitutional law regarding the healthcare system. Any private activity that has profit or earned income as its goal is considered employment in the private sector. As a result, the area of application is quite broad. And it appears even broader when one brings to mind that employment in the private sector encompasses every level of this activity – i.e., not only the prerequisites for work (training requirements, personal requirements) but also the activity itself. Article 95 of the Swiss Federal Constitution constitutes the most important basis for regulating medical professions at the Federal level. The extremely important Medical Professions Law rests on this provision.

52. Adopted by popular vote, the new Article 117a, of the Swiss Federal constitution on primary medical care is in force since 18 May 2014. The Confederation and the Cantons have the duty to ensure the adequate provision of high-quality medical care that is accessible to all. They shall recognize and promote family medicine as an essential component of primary care. This new constitutional provision shall help to raise the attractiveness of family medicine for young physicians and consequently assure primary medical care. The competences from the Confederation and the Cantons basically remain the same. In the revision of the Medical Professions Law, in Article 4, paragraph 2, the wording of letter d was changed to stress primary medical care as a goal of education and skills.

53. Article 118, paragraph 1, of the Swiss Federal Constitution contains the central goals for the Federal government in health protection law. The Federal government is obligated to enact provisions for the protection of health in three areas that are themselves divided into various subareas:

> Article 118, Paragraph 2, Swiss Federal Constitution (Health Protection)
> It shall legislate on:
>
> a. the use of foodstuffs as well as therapeutic products, narcotics, organisms, chemicals and items that may be dangerous to health;
> b. the combating of communicable, widespread or particularly dangerous human and animal diseases;
> c. protection against ionising radiation.

54. As measured against the sphere of health protection as a whole – a major portion of which the cantons still provide – the listed responsibilities of the Federal government are only partial albeit very important ones of which the Federal government has made comprehensive use.

55. Article 118a, Swiss Federal Constitution was adopted by popular vote on 17 May 2009. The Confederation and the Cantons shall ensure the consideration of complementary medicine. It is a programmatic law norm with a low normative concentration and obliges the Confederation and the Cantons that complementary medicine shall be considered in the whole health care system.

56. Another new article was introduced in the Swiss Federal Constitution by popular vote. Based on this competence, the Confederation enacted the Law on Research involving Human Beings:

> Article 118b, Swiss Federal Constitution (Research on human beings)
>
> 1. The Confederation shall legislate on research on human beings where this is required in order to protect their dignity and privacy. In doing so, it shall preserve the freedom to conduct research and shall take account of the importance of research to health and society.
> 2. The Confederation shall adhere to the following principles in relation to biological and medical research involving human beings:
>   a. It is a requirement for any research project that the participants or their legal representatives have given their informed consent. The law may provide for exceptions. A refusal is binding in every case.
>   b. The risks and stress for the participants must not be disproportionate to the benefits of the research project.

c. A research project involving persons lacking the capacity to consent may be conducted only if findings of equal value cannot be obtained from research involving persons who have the capacity to consent. If the research project is not expected to bring any immediate benefit to the persons lacking the capacity to consent, the risks and stress must be minimal.
d. An independent assessment of the research project must have determined that the safety of the participants is guaranteed.

57. Along with assignment of responsibility to the Federal government, Article 119 of the Swiss Federal Constitution contains a number of important principles in the area of reproductive health and gene technology involving humans, of which the legislators are to take heed. Constitutional authority thereby substantially limits the Federal legislation's radius of operation:

Article 119 of the Swiss Federal Constitution (Reproductive Medicine and Gene Technology Involving Human Beings)

1. Human beings shall be protected against the misuse of reproductive medicine and gene technology.
2. The Confederation shall legislate on the use of human reproductive and genetic material. In doing so, it shall ensure the protection of human dignity, privacy and the family and shall adhere in particular to the following principles:
   a. All forms of cloning and interference with the genetic material of human reproductive cells and embryos are unlawful.
   b. Non-human reproductive and genetic material may neither be introduced into nor combined with human reproductive material.
   c. The procedure for medically-assisted reproduction may be used only if infertility or the risk of transmitting a serious illness cannot otherwise be overcome, but not in order to conceive a child with specific characteristics or to further research; the fertilization of human egg cells outside a woman's body is permitted only under the conditions laid down by the law; no more human egg cells may be developed into embryos outside a woman's body than are required for medically-assisted reproduction.
   d. The donation of embryos and all forms of surrogate motherhood are unlawful.
   e. The trade in human reproductive material and in products obtained from embryos is prohibited.
   f. The genetic material of a person may be analysed, registered or made public only with the consent of the person concerned or if the law so provides.
   g. Everyone shall have access to data relating to their ancestry.

58. In June 2015, lit. c of the present article was changed by popular vote. Before the mentioned date, it was only allowed to develop as many human egg cells into embryos outside a woman's body, as were capable of being immediately implanted. Now it is permitted to develop as many human egg cells into embryos, as are necessary for medically assisted reproduction. By this innovation, the basis for the realization of preimplantation diagnostics in Switzerland was created. In June 2016, the Federal Act on Medically Assisted Reproduction (FMedG) was adapted in the way that it allows preimplantation diagnostics explicitly under particular circumstances.

59. Transplant medicine has made great advances in the past few decades. The regulation of transplant medicine in twenty-six distinct cantonal bodies of regulations was therefore no longer appropriate – among other reasons, because there were too few donor organs available and a nationwide exchange of organs was necessary. It was for this reason that in 1999 the people transferred regulation of transplant medicine to the Federal government. The Transplantation Law, which the Federal government drafted, went into force on 1 July 2007:

Article 119a of the Federal Constitution (Transplant Medicine)

1. The Confederation shall legislate in the field of organ, tissue and cell transplants. In doing so, it shall ensure the protection of human dignity, privacy and health.
2. It shall in particular lay down criteria for the fair allocation of organs.
3. Any donation of human organs, tissue and cells must be free of charge. The trade in human organs is prohibited.

60. The authority granted legislators in Article 119a, paragraph 1, of the Swiss Federal Constitution is extensive. As gathered from the paragraph's wording, it constitutes a binding legislative mandate that the Federal government has meanwhile fulfilled. According to the Transplantation Law, the cantons have no appreciable authority apart from their power of enforcement.

61. Along with the aforementioned areas of Federal authority, all further regulatory powers granted the Federal government in health-related social insurance sectors are of significance, for example, Article 59, paragraph 5, and Articles 111–113 and 116 of the Swiss Federal Constitution. The power to enact provisions for the protection of employees (Article 110, paragraph 1 lit. a, BV) also has a connection to the health system, since the country's work protection law in essence serves to protect the health of employees.

C. Cantonal Powers in the Area of Health

62. Even if those questions at the focus of public discussion are regulated at the Federal level (e.g., reproductive medicine, gene technology), the cantons still have a large number of health-related legal obligations to fulfil. But these are less easy to systematically describe than those at the Federal level – which in no way belies the fact that the cantons play a leading role in terms of not only enforcement but also in relation to the financial burdens of health law.

1. Health Supervisory Authorities

63. If one subsumes under the rubric 'health supervisory authorities' all those police regulations that aim to directly or indirectly protect human health, it becomes evident that they make up a substantial portion of cantonal legislation. In one form or another, most cantonal norms have a relation to health protection. But if one conceives a somewhat narrower definition of health supervisory authorities and concentrates on the core areas of health law, then one might point to training and licensing provisions for health personnel who are not physicians (as of 1 January 2004, the paramedical professions have been subsumed under the Federal government's Occupational Training Law), the funeral industry, the provisions addressing transplantations, and (just recently) the provisions on medicinal substances. Despite the great importance of health supervisory authorities at the cantonal level, there has been a tendency towards centralization of the various regulatory areas at the Federal level.

2. Healthcare

64. A considerable portion of the cantonal budget is spent on ensuring cantonal healthcare, in particular on the building and operation of inpatient infrastructures (hospitals, rehabilitation clinics, nursing homes, etc.). Although the KVG restricts the cantons' ability to determine the degree to which they want to ensure care, their planning autonomy is still considerable (see Articles 39 and 49, KVG).

3. Cantonal Social and Health Politics

65. Despite the national powers that allow the Federal government to enact social security laws, important aspects of social policy are still in the hands of the cantons (e.g., social benefits). It is in this context that cantonal healthcare policy must be understood. In terms of social policy, it is important if and to what extent a canton invests in inpatient infrastructure and other areas of healthcare, since the individuals who are financially better off can use non-cantonal facilities (additional private insurance, direct payers), whereas those who are less well off depend on the infrastructure maintained by the canton. To no insignificant degree, cantonal health policy equates with cantonal social policy.

66. The areas in which Federal law modifies cantonal powers (e.g., the lowering of health insurance premiums) should also be seen within the context of cantonal social policy. It is precisely in the lowering of premiums that the cantons should to a certain degree determine for themselves to what extent they wish to lower these premiums for their citizenry.

D. *Target Norms*

67. A description of authority structures alone says little about the goals of health policy and health law. As a rule, the goals of health policy either arise from principled or target norms or are tacitly assumed to be essential components of the duties of the state.

1. International Level

68. International convention law increasingly aims to specify goals for states in their attainment of the best possible healthcare. Along with those target norms that first and foremost protect certain population groups (e.g., International Labour Organization [ILO] conventions for the protection of employees), one should also mention the international guarantees of human rights.

69. The Universal Declaration of Human Rights – passed by the General Assembly of the United Nations (UN) on 10 December 1948, and from which no individual claims can be directly derived – obligates states to provide needed medical care for individuals (Article 22, paragraph 1). The health-law-relevant provisions are more concretely worded in the UN Covenant on Economic, Social and Cultural Rights (UN Covenant I) and the International Covenant on Civil and Political Rights (UN Covenant II). But this latter document – in contrast to national constitutional law and the guarantees of the European Court of Human Rights (ECHR) – contains no guarantees in the sphere of health law that go further than the aforementioned ones.

70. The central provision for health law is Article 12 of the UN Covenant I:

1. The States Parties to the present Covenant recognize the right of everyone to the enjoyment of the highest attainable standard of physical and mental health.
2. The steps to be taken by the States Parties to the present Covenant to achieve the full realization of this right shall include those necessary for:
   a. The provision for the reduction of the stillbirth-rate and of infant mortality and for the health development of the child;
   b. The improvement of all aspects of environmental and industrial hygiene;
   c. The prevention, treatment and control of epidemic, endemic, occupational and other diseases;
   d. The creation of conditions which would assure to all medical service and medical attention in the event of sickness.

71. This means that the provisions contain an actual health policy programme that encompasses not only health protection but also healthcare. One cannot derive individual claims from the provision due to its formulation and owing to the restrictive practices of bodies such as the Swiss Federal Tribunal. But in the UN Covenant

I, the contracting states are obligated to a progressive implementation of the objectives (Article 2, paragraph 1, UN Covenant I).

72. A programme adapted to the health needs of children is also contained in Article 24 of the UN Convention on the Rights of the Child, an article that applies to Switzerland without reservation:

(1) States Parties recognize the right of the child to the enjoyment of the highest attainable standard of health and to facilities for the treatment of illness and rehabilitation of health. States Parties shall strive to ensure that no child is deprived of his or her right of access to such healthcare services.
(2) States Parties shall pursue full implementation of this right and, in particular, shall take appropriate measures:
   (a) to diminish infant and child mortality;
   (b) to ensure the provision of necessary medical assistance and healthcare to all children with emphasis on the development of primary healthcare;
   (c) to combat disease and malnutrition, including within the framework of primary healthcare, through, *inter alia*, the application of readily available technology and through the provision of adequate nutritious foods and clean drinking-water, taking into consideration the dangers and risks of environmental pollution;
   (d) to ensure appropriate prenatal and postnatal healthcare for mothers;
   (e) to ensure that all segments of society, in particular parents and children, are informed, have access to education, and are supported in the use of basic knowledge of child health and nutrition, the advantages of breastfeeding, hygiene and environmental sanitation, and the prevention of accidents;
   (f) to develop preventive healthcare, guidance for parents, and family-planning education and services.
(3) States Parties shall take all effective and appropriate measures with a view to abolishing traditional practices prejudicial to the health of children.
(4) States Parties undertake to promote and encourage international cooperation with a view to achieving progressively the full realization of the right recognized in the present article. In this regard, particular account shall be taken of the needs of developing countries.

73. The UN-Disabilities Convention, entered into force in Switzerland in 15 May 2014, stipulates similar goals, adapted for the needs of disabled persons, in Article 25 (Health).

74. The Council of Europe has drafted convention law in various areas relevant to health law. But those paragraphs bearing upon medical care in the European Social Charter of 1961 and the European Code of Social Security for the Council of Europe's Member States have no application to Switzerland. In the first place, Switzerland never ratified the charter, and in the second, it had similar reservations about the European Code of Social Security.

75. But within the framework of health-law issues, certain of the ECHR provisions take on importance, in particular Article 2 (the right to life), Article 3 (the ban on torture and inhumane or degrading treatment and punishment), and Article 8 (the protection of private and family life). The defence of one's private life is above all a sensitive problem in the area of medical treatment.

76. Because of the great mobility of people, national legislators still have only a limited area of influence. Prohibitions in one state can be easily circumvented by travelling to another. Therefore, it is all that more important that the states pledge themselves to certain common principles and present a united front to the new challenges facing them. This goal is pursued by the European Convention on Human Rights and Biomedicine (4 April 1997), which fleshes out and further develops fundamental rights in the sphere of human medicine. This was the very first international convention that laid down binding rules of law in the area of medicine. Earlier international instruments dealing with medical issues had made do with a non-binding declaration or recommendation.

77. Switzerland signed and ratified the Biomedicine Convention. As its appellation spells out, the convention's goal is to protect the dignity and identity of human life in all its forms with respect to the application of biology and medicine. It also aims to guarantee every person's integrity and other fundamental rights and freedoms (Article 1, paragraph 1, Biomedicine Convention). The convention thus covers human medicine in the widest sense of the term, in particular transplant medicine (along with xenotransplantations), gene technology in the human sphere, cloning, and in vitro fertilization. It is immaterial whether the focus is on practical application – i.e., diagnostic, therapeutic, or preventative measures – or the sphere of human research.

78. Human life is assigned primacy as the fundamental substantive norm in Article 2 of the Biomedicine Convention. The interests and well-being of (individual) human lives have priority over the interests of society's interests or those of science. Hence, the contracting states are obligated to provide equal access to adequate quality healthcare (Article 3, Biomedicine Convention). Protection of an individual's desires ranks very high: In principle, in the health sphere, a procedure may only be carried out after the person concerned has been briefed and has given his or her free assent (Article 5, paragraph 1, Biomedicine Convention). The convention has special provisions for the protection of persons who are incapable of giving their free consent and for persons with psychological illnesses. In view of the rapid progress of gene technology, a crucial provision is the one that prohibits all forms of discrimination against a person due to his or her genetic inheritance (Article 11, Biomedicine Convention). In a rudimentary fashion, the convention also regulates the main lineaments of scientific research on humans (particulars are contained in a supplementary protocol). It concludes with guidelines for transplant medicine and the prohibition on profit in the use of body parts extracted from humans.

2. National Level

79. Article 41, paragraph 1b, of the Swiss Federal Constitution prescribes that the Federal government and the cantons must provide all the care necessary to a person's health. This is seen as a supplement to private initiative and the responsibility every person must take for him- or herself. The term 'health' encompasses not just the care provided in cases of sickness but all those aspects that might impair a person's health. Along with the necessary care, prevention is also an aspect of health in the sense of its being a social objective. Article 41, paragraph 1b, of the Swiss Federal Constitution must also be interpreted in light of Article 12 of the UN Covenant I, which prescribes a comparable goal to the contracting states.

80. Along with the social objective, there are further programmatic norms in the applicable constitutional law, above all Article 118, paragraph 1, of the Swiss Federal Constitution. These norms obligate the Federal government, within the framework of its constituted powers, to effect measures to meet certain standards of health protection, that is, protection against any direct impairment of a person's health. Furthermore, mere indirect impairments – e.g., through the conduit of air or by way of excessive noise – are comprised within the environmental protection Article 74 of the Swiss Federal Constitution.

81. Since 17 May 2009, the Swiss Federal Constitution has had a supplementary norm for a certain medical focus. The Swiss Federal Constitution's new Article 118a reads as follows: 'The Confederation and the Cantons shall within the scope of their powers ensure that consideration is given to complementary medicine.'

82. The cantons are free to enact target norms that go even further with regard to health, but it would appear that they have made only restrained use of this authority to date. Insofar as the state's protective duties arise from them, fundamental rights can likewise be understood as advanced target norms.

E. Interplay of Regulatory Levels

83. In conclusion, one can summarize by saying that from international law the Swiss legislators can above all derive target norms that, depending on their respective spheres of competence, can be implemented by Federal or cantonal legislatures.

84. The Federal government possesses no comprehensive authority to impose regulations in the sphere of health, but it has extremely important partial powers. The most significant of these is Federal authority in the sphere of health insurance. The Federal government's healthcare policy is managed by means of health insurance. Moreover, Federal legislation in the area of health insurance has direct repercussions on cantonal legislation.

85. The regulation of legal questions in the sphere of health is very complex in numerous areas because the law must be simultaneously applied at various levels. For example, any treatment in a public hospital operated by a municipality must take into account the Federal government's Medical Professions Law and the KVG, the specific canton's health legislation, and, if need be, those particular communal regulations applicable to that hospital.

III. Financing the Healthcare System

86. In 2013, the costs of the Swiss healthcare system amounted to Swiss Franc (CHF) 69,226.7 million, which was 10.9% of the country's GDP. According to the definition of the Federal Office of Statistics, these costs include funds connected with production and use of the Swiss healthcare system's goods and services in the course of a single year. But this is a definition that hardly encompasses the healthcare system's total costs. It does not include short- and long-term reimbursements for loss of income (daily disability and retirement benefits). This explains the importance of health insurance. Its characteristic benefits – patient care benefits – are particularly relevant.

87. The health and social system is that branch of Switzerland's economy with the most jobs. A total of 14% of Switzerland's employees are active in this sector, which means over 541,000 people in total. The percentage of the GDP devoted to healthcare costs decreased in the period 2005–2007, but this was due not to a reduction of health costs but to an increase in the GDP. From 2008 to 2009, the health costs increased massively and continued to increase steadily. In fact, health costs have steadily increased over the past ten years – on average of 4% per annum. If one compares Switzerland's health costs as a percentage of its GDP with other nations, it is with 10.9% the fifth most expensive healthcare system in the world. The United States with 16.4% are on the first place.

88. Private households bear nearly two-thirds of the economic burden, whereas the remaining third is assumed by the state (approx. 32.7%) and businesses (approx. 6.3%). Viewed from an international perspective, the great financial burden borne by private households is striking. This is due, among other things, to the fact that the most important social security system in the health sphere, compulsory health insurance, is only indirectly financed by the state through the reduction of premiums. The (great) burden of premiums for compulsory health insurance is the central reason for the heavy costs borne by private households. Other reasons are the largely private financing of dental costs and the demands of nursing care shouldered by private households.

89. Another breakdown of the financing shows that some 44% of total healthcare costs are financed by health insurance, and of that 83.5% – or about 36.7% of total costs – is covered by the compulsory health insurance (social insurance) and the remainder from additional private insurance sources. The remaining types of social insurance – old age and disabilities insurance, accident and military insurance, as well as social welfare benefits – account for about 11% of the costs. Added to this are contributions from the state (20.2%) and the costs incurred by private households outside the social security system ('out of pocket' – 18%).

90. Approximately half of the CHF 69 billion go to inpatient facilities – i.e., to hospitals (36.5%), nursing homes (13.3%), and institutions for the handicapped (4.1%). Emergency inpatient care is the source of approximately two-thirds of these costs. Outpatient treatment in hospitals makes up some 25% of the whole outpatient therapies. The remaining 5% go to rehabilitation.

91. Outpatient providers have a very strong presence, comprising about one-third of the costs. Among outpatient providers, doctors constitute the largest group.

92. The hospitals are primarily financed through direct state payments and direct payments by the various social insurance plans. Direct state payments make up some 33%; direct social insurance payments constitute some 45%. The remaining costs are assumed by private insurance companies and private households.

§3. Sources of Medical Law

I. Sources of Law at the National and International Levels

93. The most important legal sources to be heeded at the international level have already been mentioned in the description of the Swiss healthcare system.

94. As described, the Federal government is only responsible for health legislation in certain areas and has largely exhausted its powers. The core legal sources in important areas can be found at the Federal level. The following laws are the most important:

- *Bundesgesetz vom 23. Juni 2006 über die universitären Medizinalberufe (Medizinalberufegesetz)* (Federal Law of 23 June 2006 on Academic Medical Professions [Medical Professions Law]).
- *Bundesgesetz vom 18. März 2011 über die Psychologieberufe (Psychologieberufegesetz)* (Federal Law of 18 March 2011 on Professions in Psychology [Psychological Professions Law]).
- *Bundesgesetz vom 28. September 2012 über die Bekämpfung übertragbarer Krankheiten des Menschen (Epidemiengesetz)* (Federal Law of 28 September 2012 on the Combating of Infectious Diseases [Epidemics Law]).
- *Bundesgesetz vom 3. Oktober 1951 über die Betäubungsmittel und die psychotropen Stoffe (Betäubungsmittelgesetz)* (Federal Law of 3 October 1951 on Narcotics and Psychotropic Substances [Narcotics Law]).
- *Bundesgesetz vom 15. Dezember 2000 über Arzneimittel und Medizinprodukte (Heilmittelgesetz)* (Federal Law of 15 December 2000 on Pharmaceuticals and Medicinal Products Law [Pharmaceuticals Law]).

- *Bundesgesetz vom 8. Oktober 2004 über die Transplantation von Organen, Geweben und Zellen* (*Transplantationsgesetz*) (Federal Law of 8 October 2004 on the Transplantation of Organs, Tissues and Cells [Transplantation Law]).
- *Bundesgesetz vom 18. Dezember 1998 über die medizinisch unterstützte Fortpflanzung* (*Fortpflanzungsmedizingesetz*) (Federal Law of 18 December 1998 on Medically Supported Reproduction [Reproductive Health Law]).
- *Bundesgesetz vom 19. Dezember 2003 über die Forschung an embryonalen Stammzellen* (*Stammzellenforschungsgesetz*) (Federal Law of 19 December 2003 on Research into Embryonic Stem Cells [Stem Cell Research Law]).
- *Bundesgesetz vom 30. September 2011 über die Forschung am Menschen* (*Humanforschungsgesetz*) (Federal Law of 30 September 2011 on Research involving Human Beings [Human Research Law]).

95. All of these laws are in part supplemented by comprehensive ordinances.

96. The great importance of KVG and the remaining social insurance laws has already been emphasized with respect to the coverage they provide for health impairments.

97. Of particular importance are civil law and the Federal government's penal law. In the area of medicine, private law is applicable to all legal relationships in the area of medicine that are governed by such law. The areas of penal law that are of relevance here, especially the typical crimes of medical law such as personal injury and breaches of doctor-patient confidentiality, are regulated at a Federal level.

II. Sources of Law at the Cantonal Level

98. The cantons play a central role in the Swiss health system, as many important questions are regulated at the cantonal level. Along with the aforementioned spheres (see General Introduction, §2.II.C.), one must above all mention the laws on the rights of patients, some of which are quite detailed. These laws regulate the relationship between doctors and patients in both hospitals and private practices.

99. Cantonal health legislation is also important for the licensing of doctors who are not self-employed. Above all, cantonal health laws also regulate whether modern forms of service provision (group medical practices) are permitted and specify the conditions.

III. Municipal Law

100. In the health system, communal law also plays a role. In particular, it is frequently the municipalities that – alone or with other townships – operate hospitals and other expensive inpatient facilities. As long as cantonal law grants them the appropriate latitude, they may also pass laws in this area, above all hospital regulations and other norms related to the operation of these facilities.

101. Moreover, in certain cantons, the municipalities are responsible for the organization of non-hospital care and can establish norms in this area.

IV. Professional Regulations

102. The statutes of professional medical organizations, particularly the by-laws of the Society of Swiss Doctors and its subdivisions, play an important role in medical practice. Nevertheless, they are not considered objective law and are only of relevance to members of these professional societies. We will come back to this later (Part I, Chapter 4, §4).

103. Nor do the various (important) guidelines of the Swiss Academy of Medical Sciences constitute objective law. Nevertheless, they do carry some weight. In legal questions pertaining to penology and accountability, these guidelines frequently constitute guiding principles by which to judge whether the standards and restraints of medical science have been held.

§4. Health Insurance

104. When Swiss legislators passed the KVG, they sought to tackle two central issues. On the one hand, they wanted to strengthen solidarity among the insured and, on the other, to create an efficient system that guaranteed high-quality service at an affordable rate for the entire resident population.

105. The current KVG first went into effect in 1996 and has since then undergone several revisions. Additional reforms, some of which are quite far-reaching, are presently under discussion as a result of rising costs in the healthcare system.

I. A Social Insurance Based on the Principle of Solidarity

106. The health insurance programme has been conceived as a social insurance programme that provides the entire population with comprehensive coverage against the social risk of illness (see Article 41, paragraph 1b, and Article 41, paragraph 2, BV).

107. A primary objective was to strengthen solidarity between the sick and the healthy, and to this end, legislators took the following measures:

- Mandatory coverage was introduced for the entire country. The entire resident population is now not only entitled but also obliged to join this community, which is based on the principle of mutual solidarity. No one is exempt.
- The insured may freely choose and switch between health insurance providers. Health insurers must accept every person seeking insurance – regardless of their

health, age, or gender. Reservations about providing insurance, waiting periods, and other obstacles have been eliminated.
- The sick and the healthy essentially pay the same premiums ('single premium'). Insurers are in principle forbidden to tier insurance based on factors indicating a greater risk of illness, such as gender and age (with the exception of children and young adults, see Article 61, paragraph 3, KVG).
- A comprehensive legal list of benefits was created that is binding for health insurers. The benefits are the same for everyone insured by the programme.
- The economic situation of the insured plays no role in setting the single premium. The danger that the economically weak will be unable to pay their insurance premiums makes additional solidarity between the rich and poor necessary. The KVG provides for contributions from public authorities to reduce premiums when there is an economic need to do so (Articles 64 et seqq., KVG).

II. High Quality at an Affordable Rate

108. In addition to strengthening solidarity, legislators focused on containing costs, which can be achieved in two different, even contradictory, ways: through more competition or through greater state regulation. The framers of the law did not come down clearly on the side of either a free-market or a state-directed model, but instead created a system based on competition and regulation.

109. From the perspective of health economics, the health insurance market doubtless requires a certain degree of regulation. First, there is a danger that the sick will be shunned by insurers and become concentrated in the hands of a single insurer ('adverse selection'). Second, the existence of insurance in itself creates false incentives for the insured, leading them to use more services than they normally would if they were uninsured ('moral hazard').

110. Legislators have introduced a broad set of state regulations alongside the elements of competition, and the balance of power between the market and state is the subject of ongoing political debate.

111. As far as the health insurers go, the KVG primarily relies on competition. Social health insurance is provided by a body of insurers whose numbers are not restricted by law. They compete for the business of the insured, who can freely choose and switch between them (full freedom of trade). This promotes competition, but the state intervenes in the market as a strong regulator by barring risk-based premiums and by legally defining the list of services covered by the programme.

112. As for the healthcare providers, the state mainly relies on the instruments of a planned economy. Although the insured may in principle freely choose their care providers (Article 41, KVG), the system is not based on true competition because the care providers' costs are borne by the insurers rather than the insured. In fact, the large number of care providers increases costs since demand from the insured expands with the greater supply (supply-driven market): The insured have neither a financial incentive nor the necessary knowledge to apply pressure to the care providers so that they will work more efficiently.

113. Insurers are not allowed to select the care providers with whom they cooperate ('obligation to contract'). It is the state and not the insurers that determines the care providers who are authorized to charge services to the social health insurance scheme. The cantons are even legally required to conduct demand-driven planning for hospitals and nursing homes (Article 39, KVG).

114. Otherwise, care providers and insurers are accorded a high degree of autonomy in negotiating rates. They can generally negotiate the care providers' rates themselves, but the rates they agree on must be approved by the authorities.

III. The Insured

115. The health insurance programme is a people's and not a class-based insurance. Coverage is basically compulsory for the entire resident population and not limited to certain groups (e.g., employees). One of the main criteria is a person's residence as defined under civil law, irrespective of nationality (Article 3, paragraph 1, KVG; Article 1, paragraph 1, Health Insurance Ordinance; Article 13, paragraph 1, General Section of the Social Insurance Law). Under civil law, a person's legal residence is that place where he or she intends to reside permanently and that is at the centre of his or her vital interests.

116. Exceptions exist to this practice of linking insurance to a person's civil-law residence. On the one hand, certain individuals domiciled in Switzerland are not required to participate in the compulsory insurance programme (Article 3, paragraphs 2 and 4, KVG). These individuals include people who already have adequate insurance coverage through another domestic or a foreign social insurance programme. On the other hand, some individuals are subject to the compulsory health insurance even though they are not domiciled in Switzerland (Article 3, paragraph 3, KVG), such as foreign nationals with a temporary residence permit. In this case, the decisive criteria are their place of work or their place of habitual residence (Article 3, paragraph 3a, KVG). Such exceptions are defined in detail in Articles 1 to 6 of the *Verordnung über die Krankenversicherung* (KVV), or Health Insurance Ordinance.

117. The provisions in state treaties may also be applicable. For instance, within the scope of the Agreement on the Free Movement of Persons, which Switzerland signed with the EU/EFTA, the country of employment and family insurance are the relevant criteria for health insurance. According to the former principle, insurance coverage is essentially dependent on the place of work and not on the place of residence. According to the latter, non-employed family members must be covered by the insurance of the employed person. Since both principles are alien to the health insurance scheme in Switzerland, its legal framework had to be adapted accordingly.

On the one hand, the legal obligation to be insured needed to be expanded to include, for example, people working in Switzerland but living in the EU/EFTA; on the other, this obligation needed to be restricted to exclude, for example, Swiss residents working in the EU/EFTA.

IV. Premiums and Deductibles

118. The health insurers set insurance premiums, but these must be approved by the Swiss Federal Council (Article 61, paragraphs 1 and 5, KVG). Insurers essentially collect the same premium from all the insured (the so-called *Einheitsprämie*, or single premium; Article 61, paragraph 1, KVG). With just a few legal exceptions, insurers are not permitted to set premiums based on risk or income.

119. The law permits the following premium tiers:

- A tier based on the insured party's place of residence (Article 61, paragraph 2, KVG): the premiums may vary according to canton and region.
- A tier based on the insured party's age (Article 61, paragraph 3, KVG): premiums for persons up to the age of 18 (children) must necessarily be cheaper than those for older people (adults). In addition, insurers are permitted to reduce premiums for people up to the age 25 (young adults). With the exception of these regulations, age may not play role in determining premiums.
- A tier based on the selected insurance model: lower premiums may be granted for special forms of insurance pursuant to Article 62, KVG.
- A tier based on insurance coverage: premiums may be lower for insured parties without accident coverage (Article 8, paragraph 1, KVG, Article 91a, KVV).

120. Premiums must basically be paid by the insured, normally on a monthly basis and in advance (Article 90, KVV). If a person falls behind with payment, he or she is subject to the provisions in Article 64a of the KVG, which describe the legal consequences of not paying premiums (and thus sharing costs). Some of these are quite severe. If required, insurers may recover back premiums in a procedure designed to enforce their claims (Article 64a, paragraph 1, KVG). The insured are not permitted to switch insurers as long as they are in arrears (Article 64a, paragraph 6, KVG; Article 105l, KVV), but they may also not be dropped by the insurer. The insured are still required to have health insurance coverage and pay premiums despite the fact that they must essentially pay for services themselves until they settle their accrued debts. The cantons' welfare law and basic constitutional rights (Article 12, BV) apply.

121. In order to prevent the insured from making excessive use of services covered by health insurance ('moral hazard'), the insured are required to pay a part of the costs themselves (Article 64, paragraph 1, KVG). The law provides for various forms of cost-sharing, and a common feature to all is that they are not tiered according to the economic circumstances of the insured:

- Deductible (called a 'franchise'): This is the fixed annual sum the insured must pay before insurance kicks in (Article 64, paragraph 2a, KVG). It currently amounts to a minimum of CHF 300 per calendar year.
- Co-payment: The insured are required to pay 10% of the costs exceeding the deductible (Article 64, paragraph 2b, KVG). This co-payment is limited by law and currently capped at CHF 700 a year.
- Cost-sharing in the event of a hospital stay (Article 64, paragraph 5, KVG): A patient's contribution to the costs of a hospital stay is currently set at CHF 15 per day.

122. Cost-sharing by children is subject to a number of restrictions. Children are not required to pay a deductible and they need only pay half the highest permissible yearly co-payment (Article 64, paragraph 4, KVG). Furthermore, they normally do not have to pay the daily contribution to the costs of a hospital stay. If several children in a family are covered by the same insurer, their obligation to share costs is restricted even further (Article 64, paragraph 4, KVG).

123. Insurers are not permitted to impose any of the aforementioned forms of cost-sharing in the case of maternity care and after the thirteenth week of pregnancy (Article 64, paragraph 7, KVG; Article 104, paragraph 2c, KVV). This includes the deductible, co-payments, and contributions to the cost of a hospital stay.

V. Insured Risks

124. Social health insurance provides benefits in the event of illness, maternity, and accidents unless such costs are borne by accident insurance (Article 1a, paragraph 2, KVG). Health insurance is therefore not limited to the social risk of illness. For people who do not have accident coverage, it is a comprehensive insurance programme that provides benefits whenever a person's health is impaired, regardless of whether the cause is accident or illness.

125. Maternity care is also a part of the health insurance programme since pregnancy causes a need for benefits similar to the need that arises when a person's health is impaired and he or she requires diagnosis and treatment (e.g., ultrasound examinations, hospital stays). However, in the case of maternity, any loss of income after delivery is covered by the maternity compensation provisions in the *Erwerbsersatzordnung* (EOG, Income Replacement Regulations, Articles 16b et seqq.).

126. Article 3, paragraph 1, of the General Section of the Social Insurance Law defines illness as 'any impairment of physical or mental health that is not the result of an accident and requires a medical examination or treatment, or that results in the inability to work'. This legal definition contains an important medical component: the requirement that there be damage to a person's health and thus a physical or mental dysfunction. A restrictive proviso is the assumption that this dysfunction is not the result of an accident and leads to the need for an examination or treatment, or that it causes disability. These restrictions not only distinguish the concept of illness from that of an accident under Article 4 of the General Section of the Social Insurance Law but also add an objective, benefit-related component. The concept of illness is in line with the benefits offered by the social health insurance: defrayment of the costs for medical examinations and treatment as well as a daily allowance in the case of disability.

VI. Benefits

127. Health insurance basically covers the costs associated with care of the sick. This generally includes all the medical measures necessary to diagnose and treat damage to a person's health, while yet also covering services that cannot actually be described as care for the sick but that nevertheless trigger a similar need for benefits (prevention, maternity care, legal termination of pregnancies, rescue costs, etc.).

128. The most important exception to insurance coverage is dental treatment, which is covered only on a very small scale – primarily when dental disease is related to a severe general illness sustained by the insured (Article 31, KVG).

129. In addition, insurance does not cover psychotherapeutic services that are not provided or ordered by a doctor. This means that non-medical psychotherapists are currently not licensed care providers within the scope of the health insurance scheme.

130. Health insurance is based on the principle of cost reimbursement. This means that health insurers do not provide services themselves ('benefits in kind'), but only bear the costs of such services (Articles 24 and 42, KVG).

131. Article 34, paragraph 1, of the KVG directs that, within the scope of health insurance, insurers are only permitted to cover the costs of legally defined services. The lists of services drawn up by legislators and regulators are seen as exhaustive and complete. As a consequence, insurers are not allowed to provide voluntary services but must adhere to the law and legal ordinances ('principle of legality'). Private insurance may be taken out to cover additional services.

132. Furthermore, Article 34 of the KVG introduces the principle of territoriality. Insurers may in principle only defray the costs of services provided in Switzerland. Nevertheless, Article 34, paragraph 2, of the KVG and Articles 36 et seqq. of the KVV provide for exceptions to this rule, particularly if, in case of illness or maternity, there are medical reasons for having services provided abroad. Medical reasons are deemed to exist if a service cannot be performed in Switzerland and in cases of emergency (Article 36, paragraph 2, KVV). The assumption of costs is limited to two times the cost that would have been incurred in Switzerland (Article 36, paragraph 4, KVV). The criterion of territoriality has increasingly been relaxed in recent years, not only by the Agreement on the Free Movement of Persons, which Switzerland signed with the EU/EFTA (see also Article 36, paragraph 5, KVV), but also by Article 36a of the KVV, within whose scope pilot projects can apply for permission to diverge from Article 34, paragraph 2, of the KVG.

133. The principle of assistance with in-kind benefits is applicable within the scope of the Agreement on the Free Movement of Persons. Accordingly, people insured in Switzerland are entitled to benefits in kind in EU/EFTA countries if they live or temporarily reside there. These benefits are not based on Swiss law but on the regulations and modalities of the individual EU/EFTA states. The same is true if a person insured in an EU/EFTA country resides in Switzerland.

134. Article 32 of the KVG contains a blanket clause defining the central requirements for services covered by the health insurance programme. It states that these services must be effective, appropriate, and economical. If these conditions are not met, insurers are under no obligation to assume costs. Regulators only include those services on their list that fulfil these conditions. In concrete cases, care providers must always check whether the conditions are met. Article 32 of the KVG thus contains a universally valid regulation that must always be borne in mind, in both general evaluations by regulators and in assessments of concrete cases.

135. Medical services are considered effective if, from an objective standpoint, they are suitable for achieving the desired medical benefit – i.e., they have a diagnostic or therapeutic benefit, or support patient care. The central question is whether the aim of treatment (restoration or improvement of the patient's health) can be objectively achieved.

136. Appropriateness presupposes effectiveness and, as a criterion, is primarily intended to facilitate the selection of one of the available medical measures. The medical benefit of a measure is evaluated on the basis of its risks and by comparing this benefit to those of alternative measures. A measure is considered appropriate if, from an objective standpoint, it provides the best medical benefit – i.e., if it leads more quickly and effectively to success.

137. The notion of 'economical' presupposes effectiveness and appropriateness. If there are measures available with comparable medical benefits, the least expensive must be chosen. Objective criteria must be brought to bear in judgments of whether a measure is economical. Such judgments are also based on the assumption that one of several appropriate treatments will be markedly less expensive for the care provider.

138. Legislators did not content themselves with providing general criteria for services (Article 32, KVG) but went into greater detail, listing individual service categories and then the services themselves (Articles 25 et seqq., KVG). These lists are considered exhaustive (Article 34, paragraph 1, KVG; 'list principle'). The costs of services that do not appear on the lists in Articles 25 et seqq. of the KVG are not borne by the insurers. Legislators are not only authorized but also required to further define these lists (Article 33, KVG).

139. Within the scope of Article 25, paragraph 2, of the KVG, legislators have granted doctors and chiropractors a great deal of decision-making leeway. The services they provide under this Article are subject to a 'standard service assumption' (*'Pflichtleistungsvermutung'*; see also Ruling of the Federal Court [BGE] 129 V 167f, 170 [2003]). This means that the law makes the refutable assumption that care providers apply treatment methods that are effective, appropriate, and economical (Article 32, KVG). This assumption is not explicitly mentioned in the law. In Article 33, paragraph 1, of the KVG, regulators merely identify those medical and chiropractic services that are not covered by insurance or that are only covered under certain conditions. There is no genuine, exhaustive list of approved standard medical and chiropractic services ('positive list'). Rather, regulators only enumerate the medical and chiropractic services that do not fulfil the conditions of Article 32 of the KVG and are therefore not covered by health insurance or are covered only under certain conditions ('negative list' or 'exclusionary list').

140. This legal assumption plays no role in services that are not provided by doctors or chiropractors. Concerning these, regulators have both the authority and the duty to further define the lists of services described in Article 25, paragraph 2, of the KVG. They must also create exhaustive and complete lists of standard services (Article 33, paragraph 2, KVG). Health insurance only covers the costs of services appearing on these positive lists. The positive and negative lists touched upon in Article 33 of the KVG and Articles 33 et seqq. of the KVV can be found in the Healthcare Benefits Ordinance. Appendix 1 to this Ordinance contains the lists of medical services referred to in Article 33, paragraphs 1 and 3, of the KVG.

VII. Fees

141. The legal regulations on fees define the extent to which costs are assumed by health insurers. For care providers, these provisions – together with the list of services covered by health insurance – are the most important factor for calculating income.

142. The question of the amount of costs covered by the health insurance is only relevant to the legally defined standard services provided by licensed care providers who have not opted to work outside the system (i.e., those who are '*im Ausstand*'). The insured basically have a right to full assumption of costs by health insurers.

143. The fee protection provisions in Article 44, paragraph 1, of the KVG generally state that care providers must adhere to the legally defined fees. For the services they provide, they only have the right to be paid according to the fee system and may not demand additional payment.

144. The setting of fees is based on the principle of freedom of contract. In most cases, fees are specified in agreements between insurers and care providers (Article 43, paragraph 4, KVG). Consequently, the two parties have a high level of autonomy when it comes to negotiating fees, even if the agreements ultimately need to be approved by the authorities (Article 46, paragraph 4, KVG).

145. Generally speaking, inpatient services in hospitals and nursing homes are charged at flat rates, while outpatient services are subject to a combination of time-based rates and individual service fees. This type of combined system can be found in Tarif medical (TARMED), the outpatient fee schedule applicable to all of Switzerland. Under TARMED, services are converted into so-called tax points ('*Taxpunkte*'), and the amount of money for each point is fixed in negotiations between insurers and care providers.

146. Care providers who do not wish to follow to abide by the fee system may choose to work outside the system, but then they have no right to receive compensation on the basis of the KVG and they must inform any insured patients consulting them that their services are not covered by the health insurance programme (Article 44, paragraph 2, KVG).

Part I. The Medical Profession

Chapter 1. Access to the Medical Profession

§1. Training Physicians

I. Types of Healthcare Professions

147. The professions in the Swiss healthcare system basically fall into two categories: academic and non-academic. This is an obvious distinction to make since these two groups are subject to different legal foundations with respect to entry-level education, postgraduate education, continuing medical education, and professional practice.

148. The academic medical professions include those of doctor, dentist, chiropractor, pharmacist, and veterinarian (Article 2, paragraph 1 of the Medical Professions Law). The non-academic category covers all the assistant medical professions, not only including the traditional fields of midwifery and nursing but also extending to physiotherapy, ergotherapy, psychomotor therapy, and nutritional counselling as well as the occupations of medical laboratory assistant, surgical nurse, and dental hygienist.

149. The professions in psychology are positioned in between. Psychologists may choose from a great variety of educational offerings and fields of work. They may study at either state universities and institutes of applied science (*Fachhochschulen*) or at private institutions. They may work either as self-employed service providers or in the employment of doctors. On 1 April 2013 the new Law on professions in psychology came into force and resolves the problems which were discussed in the past: It protects the title of psychologist for those practitioners educated at universities and institutes of applied science and guarantees quality control.

II. Basic Principles of State Regulation

150. Healthcare professionals can damage the physical and mental integrity of the people they treat. Since the state is responsible for protecting public health, it regulates and controls educational and professional practice in these fields. Medical education, which is divided into entry-level, postgraduate, and continuing education, intersects with both the healthcare and educational systems. Consequently, both policy areas influence the way it is organized.

151. At the same time, a number of professional associations play an important role in the practical organization of entry-level, postgraduate, and continuing medical education. The new Vocational Training Law and the (Academic) Medical Professions Law explicitly grant these professional associations responsibility for educational tasks.

III. Constitutional Basis

152. Whereas cross-cantonal cooperation in the field of healthcare has made slow progress to date, an important coordinative step was taken in the field of education with the amendment to the constitutional articles on education. Referred to as the 'educational constitution', this amendment was approved by the Swiss people on 21 May 2006. The new articles transform Switzerland into a single educational space (Article 61a, BV). Although the cantons are still responsible for the school system (Article 62, paragraph 1, BV), they must now bring their systems into alignment with one another (Article 62, paragraph 4, BV). Whereas vocational training is in the hands of the Federal government (Article 63, BV), both the cantons and the Federal government share responsibility for higher education (Article 63a, BV). They are allowed to expand cooperation by entering into agreements and transferring certain powers to joint bodies (Article 63a, paragraph 4, BV). The Federal government is authorized to specify the fundamental principles of continuing education, which has become ever more important in recent years (Article 64a, BV).

153. At the Federal level, these new educational structures have primarily been defined by the Vocational Training Law, the Institutes of Applied Science Law, and the Promotion of Higher Education Law. The first two laws applied to non-academic medical professions only. The latter two laws have been replaced by the Federal Act on Funding and Coordination of the Swiss Higher Education Sector (*Bundesgesetz über die Förderung der Hochschulen und die Koordination im schweizerischen Hochschulbereich*, HFKG) on 1 January 2015. As it is the aim of this law, the confederation and the cantons have to care together for the competitiveness, coordination, and high-quality of the whole higher education sector in Switzerland (Article 1, paragraph 1, HFKG). As a consequence, in November 2015, the Federal Council remitted the bill about the new healthcare professionals law to parliament. It will regulate the competences of healthcare professionals and the license requirements of self-employed healthcare professionals.

154. The academic medical professions, which include all the doctors' professions in a narrower sense, constitute a special case. These fall under the purview of the Medical Professions Law, which went into effect on 1 September 2007. The following section focuses on these academic medical professions.

IV. Entry-Level, Postgraduate, and Continuing Medical Education

155. Entry-level education covers basic training. Postgraduate education builds on this period of basic training and is designed to deepen and broaden the acquired knowledge, skills, and capabilities with an eye towards independent professional practice. As a rule, a completed entry-level programme is required for postgraduate education. In continuing medical education, doctors update and expand their professional qualifications on an ongoing basis after completing a postgraduate degree. The purpose of continuing education is to assure the quality of professional practice.

V. Entry-Level and Postgraduate Education of Physicians within the Framework of the Medical Professions Law

156. In a total of nine chapters, the Medical Professions Law extensively regulates entry-level, postgraduate, and continuing medical education for the academic medical professions. It also deals with professional practice. These professions include those of doctor, dentist, chiropractor, pharmacist, and veterinarian (Article 2, paragraph 1, Medical Professions Law). Although the Swiss Federal Council is authorized to extend the law to include other healthcare professions (Article 2, paragraph 2, Medical Professions Law), it has not yet availed itself of these powers. An ongoing revision of the Medical Profession Law aims to adapt it to changes in the international and national legal situation, but the structure of the law will not be changed by this revision. A first part of the revision, especially regarding primary care and complementary medicine, entered into force by January 2016.

A. Entry-Level Education

157. Human and dental medicine can be studied in the German language at the universities of Basel, Bern, and Zurich, and in French at the universities of Lausanne, Fribourg, and Geneva. At Neuenburg University students may only study one year of medicine, and at the Fribourg University, they may study up to their intermediate exams (‘*Vorklinikum*’). Afterwards they must continue at one of the other universities. Most of the students from Fribourg transfer to Bern, and most from Neuenburg go to Lausanne or Geneva. Furthermore, the Polytechnical University of Zurich (ETH) will offer 100 places for medical students up to their bachelor degree in 2017. In the near future, it will also be possible to study human medicine at the University of the Italian speaking part (Università della Svizzera italiana). A programme in veterinary medicine is only available at the universities of Bern and Zurich, which have in fact merged their two departments into the Vetsuisse Faculty.

158. The universities in the German-speaking part of Switzerland (including Fribourg) introduced admission restrictions a few years ago, primarily for cost reasons. They have used a qualifying examination ever since to regulate admissions.

These universities form a pool, and all candidates are allowed to rank universities according to their preferences. These preferences are taken into account after the criterion of test results when candidates are assigned to schools.

159. The universities of Lausanne, Geneva, and Neuenburg do not limit their admissions. After the students' first year of study, an intense inner-university selection process is carried out based on the results of the first intermediary examination.

160. The Medical Professions Law contains an extensive description of the general knowledge, skills, and capabilities required for programme graduates as well as the knowledge, skills, and capabilities necessary for individual professions (Articles 6–11, Medical Professions Law). In addition to medical topics, great importance is attached to the social, psychosocial, ethical, and economic aspects of professional practice.

161. Excerpt from the Medical Professions Law:

Chapter 3*: *University Education

Section 1: *General Objectives*

Article 6: Knowledge, Skills and Capabilities

1. Program graduates must have the following knowledge, skills and capabilities:
   a. They must understand the basic principles of science necessary for preventive, diagnostic, therapeutic, palliative and rehabilitative measures.
   b. They must understand the principles and methods of scientific research.
   c. They must be able to recognise and evaluate health-supporting factors and take them into account in their professional activities.
   d. They must be able to counsel, support and care for patients in cooperation with members of other professions.
   e. They must be able to analyse medical information and research results, critically assess this knowledge and put it into action in their professional lives.
   f. They must be capable of learning from the interdisciplinary work with members of other professions.
   g. They must be familiar with the legal foundations of the Swiss social security and healthcare systems and apply this knowledge to their professional work.
   h. They must be able to judge the effectiveness, appropriateness and economic efficiency of their services and act accordingly.
   i. They must understand the relationship between the national economy, the healthcare system and the different channels through which healthcare is provided.

2. They must be able to apply these skills, capabilities and knowledge to their profession and enhance them on an ongoing basis.

Article 7: Social Skills and Personality Development

The educational programs promote the development of social skills and the students' personalities, enabling them to come to grips with future professional requirements. In particular, they enable students:

a. to recognise and respect the limits of medical practice and their own strengths and weaknesses.
b. to understand the ethical dimension of their professional activities and their responsibility to individuals, society and the environment.
c. to protect their patients' right to self-determination within the scope of treatment.

162. Furthermore, the law defines the occupationally specific educational objectives specific in the individual programmes. It sets the goals for human medicine, as noted in the following excerpt.

163. Excerpt from the third chapter of the Medical Professions Law:

Section 2: Occupation-Specific Educational Objectives

Article 8: Human Medicine, Dentistry and Chiropractic Medicine Graduates of the programs in human medicine, dentistry and chiropractic medicine:

a. must be familiar with those basic structures and functional mechanisms of the human body that are relevant to professional practice, from the molecular level to the organism as a whole, including all developmental stages and the entire spectrum from good health to sickness;
b. must be able to diagnose and treat the most common and urgent health impairments and illnesses arising in their field;
c. must be able to handle pharmaceuticals and medication in a professional, cost-effective and environmentally friendly way;
d. must be able to recognise the disease patterns relevant to affiliated fields and adapt their procedures to overarching problems;
e. must be able to summarise and communicate findings and their interpretation;
f. must be able to understand health problems from a holistic perspective; to grasp, in particular, the related physical, mental, social, legal, economic, cultural and ecological factors and effects; and to consider these factors and effects when solving health problems on an individual and community level;
g. must understand patients both individually and in their social context, and respond to their and family members' concerns;
h. must promote human health by acting as advisers and taking the necessary preventive and health-supporting measures in their professional fields;

i. must respect the dignity and autonomy of people, understand ethical arguments, be familiar with the ethical issues in their fields and base their professional and scientific work on ethical principles for the good of mankind;
j. have a due knowledge on methods an ways of therapy of complementary medicine;
k. are familiar with the tasks of the different experts of basic medical care and are aware of the central function of family doctors.

164. The revision minimally changed the wording of letter c and g and added the letters j and k to fulfil the duties assigned in the Articles 117a (‘*Medizinische Grundversorgung*’) and 118a (‘*Komplementärmedizin*’), Swiss Federal Constitution.

165. According to the Medical Professions Law, the organization of education is left to the universities (Article 16, Medical Professions Law), which must be accredited for the individual programmes of study. In addition to meeting the general accreditation criteria in the Promotion of Higher Education Law, these programmes must guarantee that students will achieve the educational aims specified in the law and be qualified for postgraduate education.

166. Concerning chiropractic medicine, the Swiss Federal Department of Home Affairs keeps a list of recognized degree programmes at foreign universities (Article 33, Medical Professions Law). The first full Swiss programme in this field was launched in autumn 2008 at Zurich University.

167. Throughout Switzerland, the study of medicine is now based on the ‘Bologna Model’. For a bachelor’s degree in medicine, students must earn 180 credits, which normally takes them three years. In the master’s programme, which also encompasses 180 credits and lasts three years, students must complete an elective year – ordinarily the fifth academic year – that includes a medical clerkship that lasts for at least ten months. Doctoral studies last about a year and round off a student’s medical studies, but they are not a requirement for postgraduate education. As rule, then, medical studies up to the master’s degree usually last six years.

168. Students complete their education by taking a Federal examination (Article 14, Medical Professions Law). The content and general procedure of the exam are determined by the Swiss Federal Council after consulting with the Commission on Medical Professions and the universities (Article 13, Medical Professions Law). Furthermore, the Federal Council commissions an examinations board to administer the exam (Article 13, paragraph 2, Medical Professions Law). Any complaints arising from the examination are handled in accordance with general Federal regulations. The revision will add a new Article 13a that assigns the duty to nominate an examination board to the Federal Council.

B. Postgraduate Education

169. The Swiss Federal Council determines which academic medical professions require a postgraduate degree to be practised independently (Article 5, paragraph 2, Medical Professions Law). Furthermore, after consulting with the Commission on Medical Professions, the Federal Council sets the duration of postgraduate programmes, which must last a minimum of two and a maximum of six years (Article 18, Medical Professions Law). Details can be found in the two appendices to the Ordinance on Diplomas, Education and Professional Practice in the Academic Medical Professions.

170. Of the forty-four recognized postgraduate degrees, twenty-five require specialist training lasting six years and eighteen of these degrees require training lasting five years. The shortest training period is required for the title of general practitioner (three years).

171. Article 17 of the Medical Professions Law describes the general objectives of postgraduate education:

Chapter 4*: *Postgraduate Education

Section 1: *Objectives and Duration*

Article 17: Objectives

1. Postgraduate training expands and deepens the knowledge, skills, capabilities, and behavioral and social competence acquired during the university education, enabling graduates to independently perform professional work in their fields. It enables them to:

a. make reliable diagnoses and prescribe or provide suitable therapies.
b. respect human dignity when treating patients and dealing with family members.
c. support patients until the end of their lives.
d. act independently in emergency situations.
e. take measures to preserve and support health and to prevent health impairments.
f. use the available resources in a cost-effective way.
g. cooperate with colleagues at home and abroad as well as with members of other healthcare professions and the responsible authorities in the healthcare system.
h. continue educating themselves throughout their careers.
i. understand the tasks of the different experts and their collaboration in basic medical care as well as the guiding function of family doctors and to fulfil their professional duties in this field.

172. Responsibility for postgraduate education lies with the national professional associations and other qualified organizations that are authorized to award Federal postgraduate degrees (Article 20, Medical Professions Law). These organizations must apply to the Swiss Federal Department of Home Affairs to be accredited for the postgraduate programmes they oversee. Together with an experts' commission that it appoints itself, the accreditation body named by the Swiss Federal Council (Article 48, paragraph 2, Medical Professions Law) reviews their applications on the basis of the criteria in Article 25 of the Medical Professions Law. The final decision is made by the Department of Home Affairs (Articles 28 and 47, Medical Professions Law).

C. Foreign Diplomas and Postgraduate Degrees

173. Due to the growing mobility of employees, it has become necessary for professional degrees to be easily comparable between countries as well as mutually recognized. This is not only in the interests of employees but also employers. Switzerland has therefore reorganized vocational training in order to make degrees acquired at Swiss institutions compatible with those earned in foreign countries and to profit from mutual recognition in the EU.

174. The mutual recognition rules with the EU and EFTA are of particular importance to Switzerland; however, the regulations on recognizing degrees are only applicable to regulated professions. A profession is considered regulated if an individual requires a degree, certificate, or proof of formal qualification to practise it in a certain country.

175. There are seven sectoral directives in the EU dealing with the professions of doctor, dentist, veterinarian, pharmacist, general nurse, midwife, and architect. The educational programmes for these occupations have been largely brought into alignment by the sectoral directives, which is the reason that they are automatically recognized in the EU.

176. This system was adopted in Switzerland together with the bilateral agreements the country has signed. According to Article 9 of the Freedom of Movement Agreement between the Swiss Confederation and the European Community, all contracting parties are required to take the necessary measures to mutually recognize degrees, certificates, and other documents proving formal qualification. The parties also agree to coordinate their legal and administrative regulations on access to dependent and independent employment and professional practice. Appendix III to the agreement lists the affected professions and summarizes the applicable EC directives on mutual recognition. A similar arrangement can be found in Article 22 of the Agreement on the Establishment of EFTA.

177. As a result, the professions listed in the sectoral directives benefit from a simplified recognition procedure. The other professions are subject to general directives, which means that Switzerland, as a host state, can specify additional requirements if there are differences between the foreign and Swiss educational programmes in subject areas whose knowledge is a crucial condition for practising these specific professions in Switzerland. The applicant may choose between an aptitude test and an adaption period (additional educational measure).

178. The Rectors' Conference of Swiss Universities (CRUS) is generally responsible for recognizing university degrees. However, since entry-level and postgraduate education in the academic medical professions is governed by Federal law, the Commission on Medical Professions is in charge of recognition in these fields (Article 15, paragraph 3, and Article 50, paragraph 1d, Medical Professions Law). The procedure is implemented by the Federal Health Agency.

179. If the foreign diploma or postgraduate degree is not recognized, the commission defines the conditions that must be met for acquisition of the Swiss diploma or corresponding Swiss postgraduate degree (Article 15, paragraph 4, Medical Professions Law). In the case of postgraduate degrees, it first consults with the organization responsible for postgraduate training.

180. The recognition of the diploma requires that the holder of the foreign diploma speaks at least one of the national languages.

D. Continuing Medical Education

181. Continuing medical education is not yet regulated, but it is prescribed as a professional duty (Article 40 letter b, Medical Professions Law).

E. Excursus: The Law on Professions in Psychology

182. Since 1 April 2013, the Law on Professions in Psychology is in force. It aims to harmonize the university programs and standardize general conditions of postgraduate education in the field. Through quality assurance, freedom of movement within the scope of the bilateral agreements with the EU is pursued. The law also protects the use of professional titles and defines the main characteristics of independent professional practice, including therapeutic and psychodiagnostic work, in order to improve protection of patients.

§2. Manpower Planning

I. Essentially No Need for Demand Planning

183. The state would violate the constitutionally guaranteed principle of economic freedom (Article 94, BV) if it were to undertake supply planning in the independent professions – i.e., if it were to influence the supply of medical services by qualified medical staff working in the private sector. As a matter of principle, the state is not responsible for preventing an excessive supply of such services.

184. However, in keeping with other constitutional goals, the state is obliged to provide adequate medical care for the population. Regulatory measures (i.e., support measures) would seem justified by an imminent shortage of medical services.

185. The planning for inpatient facilities (hospitals, nursing homes, etc.), which are in part funded by the public authorities, is a different matter. In such a case, budgetary reasons make demand-based planning necessary, and even the KVG calls for appropriate planning measures (Article 39, KVG). Although providers are given the economic freedom to operate these facilities outside the scope of demand planning by the state, they are then ineligible to receive state subsidies or to charge services to the public health insurance programme.

II. Restricted Admission to Universities and Shortage of Doctors

186. The main reason for the introduction of the aforementioned admission restrictions to medical programmes was the capacity problems of universities overwhelmed by the steadily increasing number of first-year students. The selection procedure is meant to ensure a high-quality university education with sufficient subject-related support for students.

187. However, admission restrictions could have an unplanned side effect on the Swiss healthcare market: The smaller number of medical school graduates could lead to a slight reduction of the otherwise high density of doctors in Switzerland. On a positive note, it could also lower healthcare costs.

188. Despite the high density of doctors in Switzerland, there are now regions where a shortage of doctors seems imminent over the next few decades, particularly in the area of basic medical care (general practitioners). This is one of the reasons that some universities have recently increased the number of admission slots. A collaboration between the ETH Zurich, the University of Basle, the University of Zurich and the Università delle Svizzera Italiana is provided to train more doctors in Switzerland. ETH Zurich plans to offer a new bachelor's degree programme in medicine for 100 students and the Università delle Svizzera Italian will offer seventy new places for students of medicine in the near future.

§3. Licensing Physicians

I. Preliminary Remarks

189. Since responsibility for providing the population with healthcare lies with the cantons, there are currently twenty-six different sets of regulations in this field. It is only in the area of the academic medical professions (doctors, chiropractors, dentists, veterinarians, and pharmacists) and professions in psychology that Federal regulations exist.

190. All the cantons have issued regulations requiring licensing for certain healthcare activities. As a rule, these activities include determining, preventing, and treating impairments to the health of human beings and animals; marketing products used to prevent, identify, or treat health problems; performing medical analyses; and treating pregnant women and assisting them in childbirth.

191. Whereas the cantons used to work with exhaustive, complete lists of possible healthcare professions, there is a growing tendency in modern legislation to identify the professions that require licensing. If no license is stipulated, health professions can be practised without them – although they are, of course, still subject to general legal restrictions (e.g., criminal law). This is primarily of relevance to professions that lie outside the bounds of conventional medicine and for which recognized professional degrees (still) do not exist.

192. Concerning the professions that involve activities subject to licensing, the cantons have passed various regulations that explain which of these professions themselves require licensing. Furthermore, the cantons have adopted different stances on whether independent and dependent practices are included. The relevant regulations can be found in the cantonal health laws and related ordinances as well as in special cantonal laws on individual occupations.

II. General Practitioners and Medical Specialists

193. The cantons are in charge of granting licenses for the independent professional practice of an academic medical profession (doctors, chiropractors, dentists, veterinarians, and pharmacists) and professions in psychology. They are also responsible for ensuring that these professionals are monitored by health supervisory authorities (Article 41 MedBG and Article 28 PsyG).

194. Concerning licensing by the health supervisory authorities, the Swiss system does not essentially distinguish between general practitioners and specialists. All require a postgraduate degree in order to practise their professions independently, and they must fulfil the other licensing conditions as well.

195. The Federal government stipulates the requirements for awarding and refusing licenses (Articles 36–38, MedBG; Articles 24–26 PsyG). It gives the cantons a certain degree of leeway in defining these requirements more precisely, particularly in defining the restrictions on licensing and requirements for professional practice (Article 37, MedBG; Article 25 PsyG).

196. A license is granted if the petitioner has the appropriate Swiss degree or if his or her foreign degree is recognized as an equivalent. Furthermore, the petitioner must be trustworthy, which means he or she cannot have been convicted of offences that cast doubt on his or her character. Finally, the petitioner must have the physical and mental capacity to guarantee proper professional practice (Article 36, paragraph 1, Medical Professions Law). The same applies for petitioners in the area of the Law on Professions in Psychology (Article 24).

197. In addition to the recognized diploma, an individual who wants to independently practise the profession of doctor or chiropractor requires a Swiss postgraduate degree or a recognized foreign postgraduate degree. According to the Swiss Federal Council, the criterion for independent professional practice is primarily economic – i.e., self-employment in one's own practice. If this view were widely accepted, standard national licensing requirements would exist only for a limited number of practitioners and doctors employed by others would not fall under the scope of the legal requirements. Furthermore, licensing for dependent work would be subject to cantonal law, which would lead to an unwanted fragmentation of the legal landscape. Since, in this interpretation, the important professional duties contained in Article 40 of the Medical Professions Law would only be applicable to some doctors, legal scholars have unanimously rejected the distinction made by the council. The decisive criterion should not be economic but independent from a medical standpoint. The revision of the Medical Profession Law widens the group of medical practitioners, so that the criterion of independent professional practice is not decisive anymore. Currently all medical practitioners working in private activity and with own professional responsibility are included. Crucial is independence and not being bound by instructions or being under supervision of a colleague. This regulation was already included in the Law on Professions in Psychology (Article 22, paragraph 1).

198. The license for independent professional practice is a police order. Upon fulfilling the legally defined requirements, applicants have the legal right to be issued the police permit. It is valid for a single person and is non-transferrable.

199. Holders of a cantonal license may independently practise their medical profession in another canton for a maximum of ninety days per calendar year without applying for a license from this canton. The restrictions and conditions attached to their license also apply to the work they do in this other canton. In addition, they are required to register with the responsible cantonal authorities (Article 35, paragraph 2 MedBG; Article 23, paragraph 1 PsyG).

200. Nor is a license required by foreign nationals who, based on provisions in state agreements, are allowed to practise an academic medical profession in Switzerland for a maximum of ninety days per calendar year without a license. Such individuals are subject only to the duty to register with the health authorities of the canton in which they wish to work. This group includes EU and EFTA citizens with medical practices in an EU or EFTA state; however, the profession in question may only be practised after the cantonal authorities have confirmed that the applicant meets the conditions for being able to work without a license.

201. The licensing requirements for the dependent activities of medical practitioners and psychologists are defined by the cantons and largely correspond to the requirements applicable to independent professional practice. However, individuals who do not work independently in a medical sense, such as assistant doctors with no postgraduate degree, are subject to special regulations.

III. Indirect Restrictions on Licensing to Charge Services to the Health Insurance

202. When approving Article 55a of the KVG on 24 March 2000, legislators created a legal framework for temporary demand planning for medical practitioners and a few other care providers. The moratorium imposed on licensing in this article was put into action in an ordinance that went into effect on 3 July 2002. Its main purpose was to contain costs and prevent a massive increase in outpatient services that could have resulted from doctors immigrating from the EU and EFTA.

203. Appendix 1 of the ordinance specifies the maximum number of medical practitioners per category and canton. The cantons have a certain degree of leeway in implementing the ordinance. They may diverge from the maximum figures or issue more restrictive regulations if there is an excess of providers. The licensing moratorium was initially limited by law to three years and then extended by an additional three years. The second extension was due to expire on 3 July 2008, but the moratorium was then extended again to 31 December 2009.

204. Since, despite various reform proposals, no other legislative solution was in sight on a political level to contain outpatient costs, parliament approved an amendment to Article 55a of the KVG on 12 June 2009 (Article 55a, paragraph 1, KVG). Modifying previously valid moratoriums, it went into effect on 1 January 2010 and will remain valid until 31 December 2011. The parliament decided to reintroduce Article 55a of the KVG by 1 July 2013, ending 30 June 2016, since there are no other measures to regulate the increasing number of medical practitioners. Also the mentioned ordinance was reintroduced by 3 July 2013 and will be valid until 30 June 2016. Furthermore, as part of the transitional solution, the Swiss Federal Council may use need as a criterion when licensing both independent and dependent care providers to charge services to the compulsory health insurance scheme. As of 1 January 2010, doctors whose only postgraduate degree was in general or internal medicines, as well as those with a postgraduate degree in paediatrics and adolescent medicine, were once again licensed to work without restriction at the expense of the social health insurance scheme. Consequently, exceptions of the restriction were connected with the postgraduate education. In contrast to the preceding restriction, the connecting factor for exception of the new regulation is a three-year practice at a Swiss post education training institute. This is problematic regarding the agreement of free movement of persons with the EU, since Swiss practitioners will normally fulfil this criterion, but foreign practitioners have to attend three years further education in Switzerland.

205. The loosening of the moratorium is a political compromise. However, even though it remedies a number of problems, it cannot be considered truly satisfactory given the fact that the moratorium has already lasted several years for certain groups of care providers. On 18 December 2015, the National Council decided not to permanently include this regulation in the law. By an urgent federal legislation, the moratorium was extended until 30 June 2019.

Chapter 2. The Practice of Medicine

§1. Different Types of Medical Professions

206. The Federal government has not only created uniform licensing requirements for the independent professional practice of the academic medical professions (doctors, chiropractors, dentists, veterinarians, and pharmacists), but it has also defined the most important professional duties. This chapter focuses on these professions.

207. It is worth mentioning at the start that the cantons may impose special professional duties on other medical professions, provided that these do not contradict the higher-level law. The following discussion must therefore be seen as incomplete in the sense that it does not provide an overview of the professional duties of this latter group.

§2. Duties within the Scope of the Medical Professions Law

208. The Medical Professions Law defines professional duties for the independently practised academic medical professions (doctors, chiropractors, dentists, veterinarians, and pharmacists).

209. Article 40 of the Medical Professions Law contains a long list of professional duties. Some of these are phrased in a rather general way and can be defined in more concrete terms by cantonal legislation, contracts governing treatment under private law, and codes of professional conduct adopted by medical associations. Nevertheless, the yardstick for assessing whether professional duties have been observed is the content of Article 40 of the Medical Professions Law.

210. Excerpt from the Medical Professions Law:

> Article 40: Professional Duties
>
> Individuals who independently practice an academic medical profession must abide by the following professional duties:
>
> a. They must practice their profession carefully and conscientiously and within the limits of the skills they have acquired in entry-level, postgraduate and continuing medical education.
> b. They must seek to deepen, expand and improve their professional knowledge, abilities and skills through continuing medical education throughout their lives.
> c. They must safeguard patients' rights.
> d. They may only place advertisements that are objective, reflect a public need and are not misleading or obtrusive.

e. They must pursue the sole aim of safeguarding their patients' rights when cooperating with members of other healthcare professions, and they must act irrespective of financial gain.
f. They must maintain confidentiality in accordance with the applicable regulations.
g. They must provide assistance in emergencies and take part in emergency service programs in accordance with cantonal regulations.
h. They must take out professional liability insurance or provide equivalent collateral based on the type and scope of the risks associated with their work.

211. The duty to practise a profession carefully and conscientiously (Article 40a, Medical Professions Law) has been phrased in a rather general way. In order to define the standard more concretely, one must take a closer look at professional practice and theory – and particularly at treatment relationships governed by private law. The same provision stresses that a medical practitioner may only act within the limits of his or her acquired skills.

212. Another professional duty explicitly emphasized in the law is that of continuing medical education throughout life (Article 40b, Medical Professions Law). However, the Medical Professions Law does not specifically state what this entails. Until the Swiss Federal Council defines this duty more precisely on an ordinance level, one must use, as a basis for interpretation, the recommendations on continuing education made by the various professional associations. However, it is important to note that a refusal to take part in continuing medical education does not justify a temporary or permanent withdrawal of a license, as is explicitly stated in the law (Article 43, paragraph 2, Medical Professions Law).

213. Even in the old law, misleading or obtrusive advertising was prohibited. Article 40d of the Medical Professions Law goes further, requiring that advertising be objective and reflect a public need. In practical terms, this means that true advertisements (print ads, etc.) and promotional information (office signs, letterheads, websites, notices in the doctor's office, etc.) may not mislead patients and that advertisements may not use aggressive, loud methods to persuade patients to undergo medical procedures that they do not objectively need.

214. Medical practitioners have a duty to provide assistance to people who urgently require medical treatment. This duty exists irrespective of whether the person in question is one of their patients or can guarantee payment of treatment (Article 40g, Medical Professions Law). It is more comprehensive than the duty to render assistance in an emergency addressed in Article 128 of the Swiss Penal Code (StGB). Furthermore, the same provision requires medical practitioners to take part in emergency service programmes in accordance with cantonal law.

215. Finally, medical practitioners have a duty to purchase professional liability insurance or provide equivalent collateral (e.g., bank guarantees) based on the type and scope of the risks associated with their work (Article 40h, Medical Professions Law). The concrete circumstances determine how high liability coverage must be.

§3. Professional Duties under Private Law and Duties in Treatment Relationships Governed by Public Law

216. The contract for treatment entered into between a private doctor and his or her patient must be seen as a mandate as defined in the *Obligationenrecht* (OR), or Swiss Code of Obligations, Articles 394 et seqq. The contractor is subject to a variety of duties that derive from statutes, case law, and legal theory. For example, from the comprehensive duty of care and support under Article 398, paragraph 1, OR, arises the physician's duty to treat patients faithfully, carefully, and to the best of his or her knowledge, to undertake treatment personally, to keep records on treatment, to provide patients with information, and to maintain professional confidentiality. Although all of these duties are also included in the list of professional duties in Article 40 of the Medical Professions Law, they have been considered in much greater detail in the practice of private law. As a result, private-law practice will continue to be of significance in this field.

217. Treatment relationships under public law, which are the usual type of relationships in state-run hospitals, are frequently subject to special cantonal laws on patients' rights or related ordinances. Although the duties they contain often correspond to those in private law, there may be occasional differences. However, the description of obligatory conduct in these laws and ordinances is especially important for clarifying liability issues in treatment relationships under public law.

§4. Professional Codes of Conduct

218. The regulations issued by professional associations also contain professional duties. Since these regulations are closely tailored to specific professions, they go into much greater detail than the duties defined by law. Even though these duties are only directly binding for members of the respective professional associations, they can be used to interpret the professional duties named in laws. Professional regulations and disciplinary law are extremely effective in Switzerland since doctors are highly organized, particularly under the umbrella of the Swiss Medical Association (FMH) (see Part I, Chapter 4, §4, and Part III, Chapter 1).

§5. Additional Duties and Rights in Professional Practice

219. A number of laws and regulations include duties for medical practitioners in addition to those discussed earlier. Although it is difficult to present a systematic overview, a few examples are:

- Compulsory registration by doctors in conjunction with efforts to fight epidemics (Articles 12 and 39, of the revised Epidemic Law which was set in force on 1 January 2016).
- Special briefing duties in conjunction with genetic examinations and reproductive medical procedures.
- The duties under cantonal law that more concretely define the professional duties in Article 40 of the Medical Professions Law, for example, the legal requirement to participate in emergency service programmes or to pay a substitution fee in the event of non-participation.
- Compulsory registration in accordance with cantonal law if a person dies under unusual circumstances that would appear to necessitate a criminal investigation.
- Registration in accordance with cantonal law in the event of serious criminal offences.

Chapter 3. The Illegal Practice of Medicine

220. Unlike laws in other countries, neither the Swiss Criminal Code nor any other Swiss law or regulation contains comprehensive penal regulations on the illegal practice of medicine.

221. The only offence described in Federal-level legislation can be found in Article 58 of the Medical Professions Law, which imposes a penalty of CHF 10,000 on persons who claim to hold an entry-level or postgraduate degree that they have not rightfully acquired. The same punishment applies to persons who create the false impression that they have completed an entry-level or postgraduate programme. However, these two offences represent only one part of the problem of illegal professional practice. Furthermore, there has been no attempt to clarify their relationship with the crimes of forgery and fraud in the StGB.

222. If a medical profession is practised illegally – i.e., if it is engaged in by a person who is not or no longer entitled to do so – then the general definitions of offences in the StGB apply. Of primary importance are offences against life and physical integrity (e.g., physical injury), which are considered to have been committed if a patient consents to a procedure on false premises. This occurs if the patient has been deceived about the putative physician's qualifications, in which case consent has no justificatory effect and the procedure is regarded as an offence against life and physical integrity. However, the act of deception is at most seen as fraud. In many cases, other crimes (document forgery, offences in the sense of Article 58, Medical Professions Law) are committed in conjunction with this type of fraud.

223. Cantonal law also contains penalties for persons who do not obtain the licenses required by cantonal law, who do not register their professional practice, or who engage in medical activities barred by cantonal law.

Chapter 4. Control over the Practice of Medicine

§1. Professional Liability

I. Civil Liability

A. General Introduction

224. The applicable liability regulations depend on the legal relationship that forms the basis of the liability claims. If a contract exists between the physician and the patient, the physician's liability is essentially based on Articles 97 et seq. of the OR, with the provisions in Articles 41 et seq. of the Code of Obligations cumulatively applicable. If no contractual relationship exists, two types of liability are possible: liability based on the management of affairs without a mandate (Articles 419 et seq., OR) and liability in tort (Articles 41 et seq., OR).

225. Independent of the basis of the claim, the facts establishing liability can be described as follows: The physician must conduct him- or herself in an unlawful and culpable manner and inflict damages on the patient. The conditions of liability are thus damages, unlawful conduct, causality, and culpability. The conditions are nearly the same for all claims, with the only significant differences arising in procedural law. The following sections first explain the individual conditions of liability and then address the specific characteristics of contractual and non-contractual liability.

B. Damages

226. The first premise for liability is that the doctor inflicts damages on the patient. Damages are defined as any involuntary reduction of the patient's assets. This reduction may result from a decrease in assets, an increase in liabilities, or lost profit. Damages must be distinguished primarily from an immaterial inconvenience. A mere impairment of the patient's enjoyment of life is considered an immaterial inconvenience rather than damages because no assets are concerned. However, under Article 47 of the Code of Obligations, if the impairment is quite severe, the patient may demand compensation ('*Genugtuung*') for such immaterial losses, which frequently arise from faulty medical procedures.

227. As for the types of damage, a rough distinction must be made between damage to property, damage to persons, and financial damage. Damage to persons plays a prominent role in doctors' liability. It is defined as the impairment of a natural person's health and includes all material losses caused by bodily injury or homicide.

228. In the case of bodily injuries, all costs that directly or indirectly result from the injury must be reimbursed under Article 46 of the Code of Obligations. The direct costs basically include the costs associated with rescue operations, transport, outpatient treatment, and hospital stays. Lawyer fees are also covered insofar as a lawyer is required to enforce a compensation claim due to the case's complexity. The indirect costs comprise, in particular, the damages arising from the patient's inability to work – i.e., the estimated loss of earnings or the costs of employing domestic help if the injured person manages a household.

229. In the case of homicide, funeral expenses must be reimbursed under Article 45, paragraph 1, of the Code of Obligations. Although everybody inevitably incurs such expenses, prevailing opinion would dictate that they be paid without consideration of possible benefits already received ('*Vorteilsanrechnung*'). If applicable, the cost of attempted treatments must also be reimbursed pursuant to Article 45, paragraph 2, of the Code of Obligations. Finally, the deceased's relatives may claim damages under Article 45, paragraph 3, of the Code of Obligations, provided that the deceased supported or took care of them and that they have lost this support as a result of the homicide. Recognized 'providers' in this sense are husbands, fathers, wives, mothers, step-fathers, sons-in-law, fiancées, siblings, and, generally speaking, common-law partners. However, the loss of the provider is recognized only if the supported person is in fact in need of support. This is assumed to be the case if the supported person is unable to maintain his or her previous living standard without the provider.

C. Unlawfulness

230. The conduct of the physician that causes the damage must be unlawful. It is considered so if it violates a single absolute right protected by the legal system. Absolute rights are personality, property, and intellectual property rights. They provide the holder with state-protected control over a particular domain and must be respected by all. It must be noted, however, that in individual cases conduct that is generally considered unlawful may be permissible – namely, when there are grounds to justify it.

231. Therapeutic medical procedures are violations of the patient's physical integrity and at times also infringe upon his or her mental integrity. Physical and mental integrity are an absolute right protected by the legal system under Articles 27 and 28 of the *Schweizerisches Zivilgesetzbuch* (ZGB), or Swiss Civil Code. For this reason, therapeutic medical procedures are in principle unlawful. However, they can be justified in individual cases if the patient has given his or her consent. For this consent to be valid, the patient must be briefed beforehand about the procedure. As a consequence, the doctor is obliged in individual cases to inform the patient about the therapeutic procedure and to secure his or her consent. Only then is the doctor's conduct considered justified.

D. Patient Briefing

232. The doctor must brief the patient on the therapeutic procedure so that the patient can provide informed consent. Among legal scholars and in case law, there is consensus that such information must be provided to the patient but disagreement as to the modality of the patient briefing, including point in time, form, and content.

233. As regards the time of the briefing, there is an agreement that it must take place before the procedure. Only then can the patient effectively consent to the procedure, since consent must be given on an informed basis. The physician must provide information early enough for the patient to have time to reach a decision. The severity of the procedure must be considered when determining the amount of 'consideration time'. For minor therapeutic procedures, the patient briefing must take place at least one day in advance of the treatment; for major procedures, the patient must be given three days to think the matter over. If it is impossible to observe these time periods – e.g., in cases of emergency – the briefing must take place as early as possible. It may only be omitted in exceptional cases and for compelling reasons.

234. As for the form of the briefing, the basic consensus is that it need not follow any particular form, and that it can be given not only in written form but also orally. However, it is important to note that a patient briefing based on a standardized written form may not always meet the content-related requirements of the individual case since it may not address specifics – or may address them only inadequately. If a standardized written form is nevertheless used, the patient must at least have the possibility of asking follow-up questions or of requesting that the physician clear up points he or she does not understand. The written briefing must also incorporate language that is clear to the patient, and the doctor must make sure that the patient understands him or her. If the language of the briefing is incomprehensible to the patient, it is invalid.

235. As for the content of the briefing, in terms of factual information, the talk must be divided into three parts: a briefing on the diagnosis, a briefing on the course of treatment, and a briefing on risk. As part of the diagnosis briefing, the patient must be informed about the medical findings, their meaning, and the diseases or ailments he or she is suspected of having. Patients can legally consent to an imminent therapeutic procedure only if they are aware of the state of their health, since knowledge of the diagnosis is of fundamental importance to all further decisions. But although the briefing about the current state of a patient's health must be clear and complete, doctors are under no obligation to inform patients of diagnoses that are suspected yet unconfirmed. Indeed, they are even forbidden to do so if it might endanger the patients' health. The briefing on the course of treatment, which follows the briefing on the diagnosis, serves to inform the patient about the type of therapeutic procedure used, its course and objective, as well as alternative treatments. The course of treatment must be explained to the patient in such a way that he or she at least has a rough understanding of it. A detailed description is unnecessary because specifics about the technical course of an operation would be overwhelming for most patients. Furthermore, patients must be told what course the illness is likely to take without the therapeutic procedure. If foregoing the procedure is an alternative worth considering, doctors must clearly communicate this to patients. The Swiss Federal Supreme Court has generally recognized a patient's right to be informed about alternative treatments, but it has left open which alternatives a doctor must explain to the patient (BGE 105 II 284, 286 et seq. [1979]). Following German doctrine and case law, Swiss legal scholars assume that, at the very least, patients need to be informed about alternative forms of treatment if the method proposed by the doctor deviates from standard treatments or if several different treatments are available and all offer the same chances for recovery. Doctors are not required to inform patients about treatment methods that have not progressed beyond the test phase. They are obliged to brief patients about new procedures only if these have become widely established. The briefing on risk takes place after the briefing on the course of treatment or regularly coincides with the first such briefing. It contains information on possible and typical complications associated with specific therapeutic procedures – complications that can arise even if doctors follow the rules of medical science. Nevertheless, doctors need not explain risks attached to every procedure and are thus known to the general public, such as the risk of general infections, post-operative incisional hernias, thromboses, and the fat embolisms that may result from more serious operations. Furthermore, doctors are not required to provide information on very-low-probability risks unless the anticipated damages are quite severe and might have a profound influence on the patient's lifestyle. However, there are no general principles governing what risks must and must not be explained. As a consequence, there is legal uncertainty in this field.

236. If the briefing is inadequate in terms of its form, content, or the time when it is given, the patient cannot validly consent to the therapeutic medical procedure, with the result that it is not justified and therefore unlawful. This holds true even if the doctor otherwise abided by the rules of medical science. The doctor is then liable for all those damages arising from the procedure even if he or she has not committed a medical error.

E. Informed Consent

237. Consent, given by the patient after being briefed, constitutes the justification for a therapeutic medical procedure that is otherwise in and of itself unlawful. Normally it is only the patient who may give consent, but if the patient is not competent – i.e., if he or she is unable to act rationally – a legal or appointed representative may give consent in his or her place, or decisions may be based on the patient's hypothetical desire. Nevertheless, representation of the patient or the assertion of his or her hypothetical desire may in principle only be considered if the procedure is medically necessary.

238. In addition to the requirement that consent be given by the person who is entitled to do so in each concrete case, it must be noted that consent is only valid if it is provided after a briefing commensurate with the requirements of the law, if the person entitled to give consent is granted sufficient time to consider the procedure, and if there exist no defects of consent as caused by error, deception, or threat. Moreover, the person providing consent must be able to revoke it at any time.

239. If the patient or his or her representative refuses to consent to the procedure, the physician is not allowed to perform it. If the physician does perform the procedure, he or she is liable under civil and criminal law. This is also true of procedures necessary to save the patient's life, since the patient's right to self-determination also includes the right to make objectively irrational decisions.

F. *Duty of Care*

240. It is important to note that consent covers only those therapeutic medical procedures that are performed with care. Careless treatment is not justified and is thus unlawful.

241. The doctor does not owe the patient successful treatment. He or she is merely obligated to take objectively careful action. In the scope of the contract for medical treatment, the physician's actions consist of examining the patient, making a diagnosis on the basis of this examination, evaluating possible treatments, selecting a treatment together with the patient, and putting this treatment into action. The physician's actions can be described as 'objectively careful' if they represent behaviour that the patient can expect of an abstractly imagined 'average' individual from the same profession. The patient can expect, in particular, that the physician has the expertise and capabilities necessary for the treatment, that he or she does all that is necessary to ensure the desired success and to protect the patient's interest in integrity, and, finally, that the treatment is performed *lege artis*, that is, in accordance with the rules of medical science and honouring all possible agreements between the physician and the patient. The rules of medical science do not, for the most part, derive from state law, but are generally defined in abstract terms in the universally recognized guidelines of professional medical organizations and specified more concretely for individual cases by the judge of the liability trial, usually with the help of an expert.

G. *Causality*

242. A natural causality must exist between the doctor's unlawful conduct and the damages suffered by the patient. It is deemed to exist if the unlawful conduct constitutes a *conditio sine qua non* for the damages or if the damages would not exist without this conduct. The natural causality must be demonstrated by the injured person, but he or she is not required to offer scientifically precise proof. It suffices if overwhelming probability speaks to the likelihood of natural causality.

243. The *conditio sine qua non* formula is valid only for active unlawful conduct. If, on the other hand, the doctor's unlawful conduct results from neglecting to perform an action prescribed by the contract or the law, the *conditio cum qua non* formula is applicable. One must now ask whether the patient would not have suffered damages if the doctor had behaved in a manner that was compliant with the law and his or her duties. This pertains above all to cases in which the doctor has not given the patient a proper briefing on the therapeutic medical procedure, but the patient would still have given his or her consent if the briefing had been comprehensive. In this case, the doctor is not liable for damages resulting from the therapeutic procedure – at least not if the procedure was otherwise carried out according to the rules of medical science (BGE 108 II 59, 62 et seq. [1982]).

244. In addition, adequate causality must exist between the doctor's unlawful conduct and the damage sustained by the patient. In contrast to natural causality, which is a question of action, the question of adequacy is a legal question. Adequate causality exists if, based on the usual course of things and general experience of life, the unlawful conduct is suitable to causing the damages. Adequacy is intended to limit liability. The doctor may only be made responsible for causal chains foreseeable at the time of treatment, in contrast to highly unlikely causal connections, which, as is only fair, cannot be attributed to him or her. According to the prevailing view among Swiss legal scholars and in case law, the question of adequacy must be judged from an *ex post* perspective – which should be criticized, since it is hardly possible for the causal chain to be evaluated as inadequate at the trial, when everyone involved is aware of the link between the unlawful conduct and the damages.

245. It is important to point out that adequate causality can be interrupted. An interruption is assumed to exist if an additional adequate cause materializes at a later date and is so important for the damages that the doctor's unlawful conduct no longer appears to have legal relevance. Personal negligence, gross third-party negligence, and *force majeure* are possible grounds for an interruption. For instance, causality between the first procedure and the resulting damages can be interrupted by a subsequent grave error in treatment (gross third-party negligence). However, an interruption of an adequate causal chain is rare because the conditions for the intensity of the additional cause are so high.

H. Culpability

246. The conduct of the doctor that causes damages to the patient must be both unlawful and culpable. The unlawful conduct of the doctor is regarded as culpable if he or she can be held morally and legally responsible for it. On the one hand, culpability presupposes that the doctor was legally competent at the time the damages occurred (subjective component) and, on the other, that he or she deliberately or negligently caused the damages (objective component). The doctor acts deliberately if he or she intentionally causes the damages or if he or she at least accepts the possibility of their occurrence. Deliberate damages rarely occur in practice. The doctor acts negligently if he or she does not observe the usual principles of care in his or her profession. A rough distinction is made between gross, ordinary, and slight negligence. A person who disregards the most elementary standards of care is guilty of gross negligence. If the individual's actions diverge only marginally from the common standards of care, he or she acts in a slightly negligent fashion. Ordinary negligence lies between the two.

247. Because standards of care are determined by objective criteria, the objective aspect of culpability differs only slightly from the duty of care, which is examined in terms of unlawful conduct. Since the subjective component of culpability (the doctor's mental competence) is ordinarily given, culpability has hardly any selective effect as a condition for liability. This is all the more true since case law affirms the doctor's liability for all violations of the duty of care, even for cases of slight negligence.

248. However, if a contract exists between the doctor and the patient – as is usually the case – liability may be limited under Article 100, paragraph 1, of the Code of Obligations in cases of slight and ordinary negligence. However, under Article 100, paragraph 2, of the Code of Obligations, the judge may regard a contractual renunciation of liability as null and void for slight and ordinary negligence if responsibility results from pursuit of a trade licensed by the authorities. Since the medical profession is among the professions licensed by the authorities, one cannot rule out the possibility that judges will nullify a contractual clause that exempts a doctor from liability for slight and ordinary negligence. Furthermore, a number of legal scholars believe that the restriction of liability for personal damages is immoral and thus invalid, since bodily integrity constitutes a valuable and legally protected interest that is incompatible with the idea of limited liability.

I. Statute of Limitations

249. Once the limitation period has been exceeded, the debtor can prevent the enforcement of the statute-barred claim by pleading the statute of limitations at the trial. Under Article 127 of the Code of Obligations, contractual compensation claims become statute-barred after a period of ten years. Non-contractual or tort claims for compensation became statute-barred one year after the day on which the injured party became cognizant of both the damages and the identity of the liable party – but at any rate, with expiration of a ten-year period beginning on the day of the harmful act.

J. Liability for Pain and Suffering (Immaterial Damages)

250. Article 47 of the Code of Obligations directs that in cases of bodily injury, the judge may, in recognition of special circumstances, award the injured party an appropriate sum of money as compensation ('*Gegnugtuung*'). The primary person eligible for compensation is the injured party him- or herself, but the prevailing view in legal literature is that the injured party's relatives may also qualify as secondary claimants, insofar as they have been affected by their relative's injury in terms of their personal circumstances.

251. For the judge to award compensation, a bodily injury must exist. This is defined in the broadest sense and may include physical impairments that do not lead to economic disadvantages and the psychological distress that can result, for instance, from an unsuccessful operation.

252. Furthermore, for the injured party, the bodily injury must result in immaterial damages such as pain and suffering. The physical or mental pain must be of a certain objectively measurable severity. This means that slight impairments of the patient's well-being do not constitute immaterial damages. Since the severity of the injured party's physical or mental pain is objectively considered, immaterial damages also exist if a person is no longer able to feel pain under the existing circumstances – if, e.g., the patient is in a permanent coma or has suffered a brain injury that greatly impairs his or her perceptions.

253. In addition to bodily injury and impairment due to pain (immaterial damages), all the other usual conditions of liability must exist – i.e., the bodily injury must be caused unlawfully, there must be a natural and adequate causal connection between the unlawful bodily injury and the immaterial damages, and the liable party must act culpably. It must also be noted that under Article 47 of the Code of Obligations, compensation can be awarded only 'in recognition of special circumstances'. Such circumstances are deemed to exist, in particular, if the liable party's culpability can be described as severe. This is why compensation is also often understood as 'private punishment'.

254. According to Article 47 of the Code of Obligations, the judge may also award an appropriate sum of money as compensation for homicide. In this case, it is the relatives of the person killed who are eligible for compensation. The conditions of liability are the same as in cases of bodily injury – the homicide must be unlawful and unjustified, it must causally produce immaterial damages or mental pain for relatives of a patient killed, and the liable party must act in a culpable fashion.

*K. Determining Damages and Compensation (*Genugtuung*)*

255. The judge has the authority to determine the type and amount of compensation for the sustained damages. According to Article 43 of the Code of Obligations, he or she must take into account the circumstances and culpability of the liable party. In the case of slight culpability, it is always possible to reduce the amount of compensation that is awarded, but in cases of gross culpability, the amount of compensation may be reduced only in exceptional cases. Aside from fault, the facts crucial to determining the amount of compensation include the financial situation of both parties. If the claimant is clearly better situated than the person liable and can easily cope with the losses, the judge may take this into account when determining compensation – provided the liable party has not acted deliberately or with gross negligence. The same is true if the liable party entered into business with the claimant without remuneration and damages have arisen from these transactions, if chance constitutes an adequate cause of the occurrence or worsening of the damages, or if the damages or their severity were unforeseen for the liable party.

256. The judge has a great deal of leeway when setting compensation. The most important factor for the determination is the severity of the injury and the degree of the doctor's culpability regarding the occurrence of the damaging event. In the case of homicide, the courts generally award relatives compensation between CHF 20,000 and CHF 40,000. In the case of bodily injury, compensation as high as CHF 100,000 has been awarded, and in any event compensation amounts have increased over recent years.

II. Criminal Liability

A. General Introduction

257. A physician's actions touch upon a variety of individual and general interests protected under the penal code, and violations of these interests can result in sanctions. As far as personal interests go, the focus is on violations of the patient's interest in preserving his or her physical and mental integrity as well as his or her own life. In terms of general interests, the breach of the duty of confidentiality is a central issue. Preservation of the patient's physical and mental integrity is protected under Articles 122–126 of the *Schweizerisches Strafgesetzbuch* (StGB), or StGB, and preservation of the patient's life under Articles 111–117. The StGB distinguishes between persons who deliberately or negligently infringe such interests. Medical criminal law revolves around bodily injury caused by negligence (Article 125, StGB) and involuntary manslaughter (Article 117, StGB). In contrast to neighbouring Austria, Switzerland has not defined unauthorized therapeutic treatment as a crime. As a result, the patient's right to self-determination is protected in criminal law by the provisions governing the crime of bodily injury. According to the prevailing views in legal literature and the decisions of the Swiss Federal Supreme Court, every violation of the patient's physical integrity is a bodily injury that satisfies the definition of a crime, even if it is performed for therapeutic reasons. As such, it must be justified by the patient's consent or by other circumstances.

B. Bodily Injury Caused by Negligence

258. Under Article 125 of the StGB, the doctor renders him- or herself liable to prosecution if he or she violates the duty of care and causally inflicts a bodily injury on the patient (physical element of the offence). A further requirement is that the doctor should not act deliberately, and it must be foreseeable by him or her that his or her conduct can cause this bodily injury (mental element of the offence). The following conditions must therefore be fulfilled for doctors to be punishable under Article 125 of the StGB: From an *actus reus* perspective, the duty of care must be violated and a bodily injury must exist; from a *mens rea* perspective, the doctor must have acted unintentionally and the bodily injury must have been foreseeable. The following sections address these conditions.

259. The duty of care is violated if the doctor acts carelessly from both an objective and subjective perspective. The condition of objective carelessness is fulfilled if the doctor's conduct does not reflect that of a conscientiously acting average member of the same profession, which is indeed the case if the doctor disregards the rules of medical science or does not properly brief the patient. In such cases, one may consult the explanations of doctors' liability under private law. Subjective carelessness exists if the doctor's conduct does not conform to the standard the patient may personally expect from him or her. The doctor's level of education and additional subjective circumstances such as fatigue, lack of time, and so forth are taken into account when defining this standard.

260. A bodily injury exists if the patient's health deteriorates by objective measure, without the patient desiring this or without his or her having validly consented to the therapeutic medical procedure and the accompanying deterioration of his or her health. The deterioration must be significant or else the doctor's action is classified as mere battery ('*Tätlichkeit*') under Article 126 of the StGB, which is only punishable if committed deliberately.

261. The causality between the violation of the doctor's duty of care and the bodily injury exists if the patient would not have sustained a bodily injury had the doctor not violated his or her duty of care. The doctor does not render him- or herself liable to prosecution if the bodily injury would also have occurred had the doctor acted with care.

262. A further condition is that the doctor should not act deliberately. An action is regarded as deliberate if the doctor knowingly and intentionally violated his or her duty. Moreover, it must be foreseeable to the doctor that his or her conduct can cause a bodily injury not covered by the patient's consent. The injury is only considered unforeseeable if unusual circumstances such as the contributory negligence of a third party or material defects jointly cause it, if these special circumstances were absolutely unexpected, and if they appear to be the most probable and immediate cause of the bodily injury not desired by the patient.

C. Involuntary Manslaughter

263. Involuntary manslaughter differs from negligent bodily injury in terms of both its outcome, that is, death, and the fact that a person cannot validly consent to being killed. Apart from this, the same conditions are applicable as those governing bodily injury caused by negligence: The doctor must have violated his or her duty of care and thereby have causally brought about the patient's death. Furthermore, the doctor cannot have acted deliberately, and the death of the patient must have been foreseeable to him or her.

III. Vicarious Liability

A. The Contractual Liability of an Auxiliary

264. Often it is impossible for the doctor to personally perform all the tasks of the contractual treatment relationship, and he or she will therefore delegate these tasks to auxiliaries or substitutes. Auxiliaries are agents who perform the tasks delegated to them under the doctor's supervision. They include such persons as nurses, orderlies, doctor's assistants, X-ray technicians, and laboratory workers. Substitutes, on the other hand, are agents who do not act under the doctor's supervision. Substitution occurs, for example, when a general practitioner requests a specialist to perform certain tasks within the scope of treatment.

265. Concerning the doctor's liability for his or her auxiliary's harmful conduct, one must first ask whether the doctor was authorized to delegate the task to an agent. This is the case if the patient has given express consent to the task being delegated. The same applies if the use of an auxiliary for a particular task – e.g., a laboratory examination – is common practice and the patient knows from the start that the doctor will involve an assistant. Furthermore, the delegation of a task to an assistant is permissible if it is immaterial for the patient whether the doctor fulfils the task him- or herself or whether he or she allows a third party to do so since the performance of the task is not dependent on the person of the doctor or, in particular, his or her expertise.

266. If the doctor is authorized to use an auxiliary, his or her liability is based on Article 101, paragraph 1, and Article 97 of the Code of Obligations, according to which the doctor is in principle responsible for damages that his or her agents cause the patient. However, this is applicable only if the agent causes damages to the patient while performing his or her official duties and if the doctor can hypothetically be held morally and legally responsible for the agent's conduct. The agent is deemed to have caused damages to the patient in the discharge of his or her official duties if the damaging action has not occurred 'on a frolic of his own', but is temporally, spatially, and functionally linked to the fulfilment of such duties. The condition of hypothetical culpability is fulfilled if the doctor could be held morally and legally responsible for the assistant's action had he or she carried it out him- or herself.

267. If, on the other hand, the delegation of a task is unauthorized, the doctor is considered to have violated his or her contractual duties and is liable for the damages resulting from this breach under Article 97, paragraph 1, of the Code of Obligations. The doctor must in principle compensate the patient for all damages that the auxiliary has caused in the scope of his or her duties. In particular, the doctor cannot argue that he or she could be held morally and legally responsible for the auxiliary's action had the doctor carried it out him- or herself.

268. One example of a doctor's liability for an auxiliary can be found in a decision by the Swiss Federal Supreme Court (BGE 116 II 519 et seq. [1990]) involving a paediatrician in the canton of Zurich and a 1-year-old child being treated by him. One night the child suffered from severe diarrhoea and vomited all it had eaten. The next morning the child's mother called the doctor's office to make an appointment but was rudely dismissed by the doctor's assistant, who merely advised her to give the child Coca Cola and orange juice and told her not to call again until four days later. Even though the child's health visibly worsened within twenty-four hours, the child's parents did not dare call the doctor. Forty-eight hours after the call, the child was unconscious and suffering from cramps, which finally compelled the parents to go to the doctor's office. The child was taken immediately to the children's hospital in Zurich, where doctors managed to save its life at the last minute. However, the child sustained severe brain damage as a result of the illness and has been in need of care ever since. The Swiss Federal Supreme Court affirmed the doctor's liability under Articles 101 and 97 of the Code of Obligations for the damages caused to the child by the conduct of his assistant.

269. Concerning liability for substitutes, a distinction must be drawn regarding whether the doctor is authorized to delegate tasks to a substitute or not. Under Article 398, paragraph 3, of the Code of Obligations, authorization exists if the doctor is given permission by the patient, if he or she is compelled by circumstance to involve a substitute, or if use of a substitute is commonly regarded as permissible. For example, the doctor may be compelled to use a substitute if it is in the patient's interests. Delegation of tasks to an agent is commonly regarded as permissible if the patient knows from the start that the doctor will be unable to perform the task him- or herself.

270. If the doctor is authorized to use a substitute, the substitute's actions may generally not be ascribed to the doctor. Rather, under Article 399, paragraph 2, of the Code of Obligations, the doctor is responsible only for exercising due care when selecting and instructing his or her agent. However, this is true only if the agent is consulted in the patient's interest; otherwise the doctor is liable under the respective first paragraphs of Articles 101 and 97 of the Code of Obligations.

271. If the doctor is unauthorized to use a substitute, he or she is liable for the substitute's actions just as if they were the doctor's own under Article 399, paragraph 1, of the Code of Obligations. This ruling is too lenient, though, since unauthorized substitution in and of itself represents a breach of contract.

B. The Non-contractual Liability of an Auxiliary

272. Physicians are subject to non-contractual liability on the basis of Article 55, paragraph 1, of the Code of Obligations. In the case of contractual liability, the doctor may only exempt him- or herself from liability under Article 101, paragraph 1, of the Code of Obligations if the doctor can prove that he or she could not be held morally and legally responsible for the auxiliary's action had the doctor performed it him- or herself. In the case of non-contractual liability for an auxiliary, though, the possibilities for exculpation are more comprehensive: The physician need only prove that he or she has proceeded with care in selecting, instructing, and supervising the auxiliary. He or she need not accept responsibility for the auxiliary's actions.

C. The Liability of an Auxiliary under Public Law

273. According to Article 61, paragraph 1, of the Code of Obligations, the Swiss cantons may legislate regulations that diverge from private law in an attempt to define the duty of state employees to provide compensation for damages they cause when carrying out official tasks. All of the cantons have availed themselves of this legislative authority and have issued cantonal laws on accountability or state liability. These laws are applicable, in particular, to cases in which patients suffer damages while being treated in a public hospital. The conditions of liability are essentially the same in all cantons and are addressed in general terms in the following paragraphs.

274. The facts establishing liability can be described as follows: A state employee must unlawfully cause damages or an immaterial inconvenience to a private person while discharging his or her official duties. Moreover, a natural and adequate causality must exist between the unlawful conduct and the damages.

275. 'State employee' is defined in the applicable liability laws. The term is ordinarily understood to include all people who are directly entrusted with public tasks. It is basically immaterial whether the person works full or part-time, whether he or she has been elected to the public service, or whether he or she has an employment contract governed by public or private law. Consequently, all employees of a public hospital are regarded as state employees.

276. The liability criteria for damages and immaterial inconvenience correspond to those for damages under civil law, including the conditions of unlawfulness and the causality between the unlawful conduct and the damages or immaterial inconvenience. The explanations for medical liability under civil law can be consulted.

277. A further requirement for compensation claims is the existence of a functional link between the state employee's harmful conduct and his or her official duty. If damages occur while the employee is 'on a frolic of his own' and not performing official duties, it does not result in liability. The decisive question is whether the state employee is put in a position to cause damages because of his or her official position. For example, if while cleaning up a hospital laboratory, a physician empties a glass of acid out the window and thereby injures a patient, a compensation claim is regarded as justified, but not if the doctor causes a fire by throwing a cigarette out the window, since in the latter case, he or she is not performing an official duty.

278. As a rule, the culpability of the government employee is not a requirement for liability, at least not in cases in which the injured party asserts a claim for reimbursement of material damages. But compensation (*Genugtuung*) is only awarded if the government employee is deemed to be culpable.

279. A distinction must generally be made between three types of state liability. In the case of exclusive state liability, the state alone is liable for damages caused by a state employee. In the case of external liability for civil servants (*'externe Beamtenhaftung'*), the state employees themselves are accountable to the injured third party. Finally, in the case of internal liability for civil servants (*'interne Beamtenhaftung'*), the state is the primary party liable for damages caused by its employees, but it can recover damages from the employee if he or she has caused the damages in a deliberate or grossly negligent fashion. The federal government and most cantons have chosen the last-mentioned model. In other words, the injured party must ordinarily assert his or her compensation claim directly against the state, and then the state, if necessary, will address itself to the employee.

§2. Quality Assurance

280. Under occupational and professional law, physicians are required to maintain quality assurance (quality and cost controls). The Federal government and the cantons may exercise a direct influence on quality assurance through social security systems. The cost and quality control regulations specified in the KVG are of special importance due to the prominent role played by health insurance in the healthcare system (for a more detailed discussion, see General Introduction, §4). The other social insurance programmes (accident insurance, military insurance, and disability insurance) also contain brief supplementary regulations on quality assurance.

281. Physicians and other healthcare providers are monitored under the KVG so as to ensure that they provide high-quality services at an affordable price. The quality and cost controls discussed in the following paragraphs are largely facilitated by the measures taken to create transparency and comparability under collective bargaining law (e.g., uniform fee structures throughout Switzerland and invoicing regulations).

282. There is a strong public interest in having healthcare providers monitored independently. As the group footing the bill, insurers, too, have a special interest in effective cost controls – yet they are unable to guarantee the necessary independence of such controls. This is why Swiss legislators have created the office of the medical examiner (*'Vertrauensarzt'*) to serve as an independent authority to ensure cost and quality control (Article 57, KVG).

283. Every insurer appoints a medical examiner (Article 57, KVG) after consultations with the relevant medical associations. Although the examiners are employed, or at least commissioned, by the insurer, they remain independent as regards professional decisions. Neither the insurers nor the healthcare providers may give medical examiners orders. Their core task lies in monitoring healthcare providers. They evaluate whether the conditions are fulfilled for the insurers to provide standard benefits. In addition, they perform advisory work. For the medical examiners to do their job properly, they require comprehensive information from healthcare providers. If necessary, they may examine insured patients themselves.

284. Article 56 of the KVG addresses the cost effectiveness of medical services. Physicians must limit themselves to services that are objectively necessary. Otherwise one speaks of '*Überarztung*', or 'over-doctoring' ('*Polypragmasie*'). There are a variety of methods for implementing cost controls, the most common being a comparison of average costs. Under this method, over-doctoring is deemed to exist if a substantial number of invoices that one doctor sends to a health insurer are noticeably higher, on average, than those from other doctors who work in a similar field and have a comparable number of regular patients. A further condition is that no special reason exists for the difference in costs. If over-doctoring has been ascertained, the insurer may refuse to pay the fee or demand reimbursement of paid invoices. It is up to insurers to enforce their claim to reimbursement through litigation.

285. Article 58 of the KVG defines quality assurance measures in the narrower sense. On the one hand, such measures include systematic scientific controls, which are conceived and implemented mainly by healthcare providers and insurers. On the other hand, the measures include controls by regulators. They may, for instance, stipulate that approval must be obtained in advance from the medical examiner for certain services or that only certified healthcare professionals are allowed to provide particular services ('exclusion from fees'). Although quality assurance was ineffectual just a few years ago, a number of initiatives have recently been introduced to enhance the programmes – not only by the Federal government and the cantons but also by healthcare providers and insurers. One example is the publication of standardized evaluations of hospital quality (infection rates, etc.).

286. If healthcare providers violate cost and quality control regulations, they are subject to disciplinary sanctions (see following discussion).

§3. Review Boards

287. Medical work is monitored by a variety of authorities. Of particular importance are the cantonal licensing and supervisory authorities, which in most cases are the cantonal health departments. They are responsible for supervising the activities in professional medical practice that are subject to licensing, for identifying violations of state professional law (i.e., professional duties), and for ordering the necessary disciplinary actions.

288. Worthy of special attention are the administrative measures that state authorities may take if the conditions for medical activities subject to licensing are not fulfilled or only partially so. The purpose of the administrative measures is not to impose sanctions on doctors for conduct in violation of professional duties but to restore public order and protect public interests. Consequently, there need not be any fault on the part of medical practitioners for them to be subject to such sanctions. For example, if a doctor's conduct undermines his or her trustworthiness, the license for professional practice may be withdrawn 'for safety reasons', regardless of fault. The reason for this is that, under the Medical Professions Law, a license to practise medicine is granted on the condition that the medical practitioner is trustworthy and can physically and mentally guarantee proper professional practice.

289. The Medical Professions Law contains a clear set of regulations on possible administrative measures pertaining to the independent practice of medicine. On the one hand, the awarding of licenses may be subject to professional, time-based, and geographical restrictions as well as to a variety of other conditions (e.g., cantonal age limits for license holders). On the other hand, licenses may be revoked by the responsible cantonal authority if licensing conditions are no longer or were never met. The withdrawal of a license applies only to the licensing canton and is not valid nationwide.

290. The cantonal authority that grants the license for professional practice is responsible for ordering administrative measures. The cantons are free to transfer these powers to cantonal supervisory authorities.

291. The regulations on quality and cost effectiveness in social insurance law are overseen by social insurance (court) authorities. Mention has already been made of the social insurance arbitration board, which rules on social insurance disputes between healthcare providers and insurers.

292. Also worthy of mention are the cantonal ethics commissions, which are required to approve research petitions in all fields of human medicine (see §4.III below).

§4. Disciplinary Organizations

I. Organization of Physicians

293. Professional associations in Switzerland do not have the same status as in other European countries such as Germany and Belgium, since they are organized under private law and do not generally perform state tasks – with the exception of the area of continuing medical education. Compulsory membership in professional organizations was abolished in the nineteenth century. Supervision of professional medical practice is divided along two lines: state supervisory authorities ensure that the law framed by the state is obeyed, while private professional organizations are permitted to enforce their own 'private' codes of professional conduct against their members.

294. The FMH is the national professional organization for Swiss doctors and the umbrella organization for cantonal and specialist medical societies. It is organized as an association under private law in accordance with Articles 60 et seqq. of the ZGB. Self-employed physicians and doctors in the employment of others are allowed to join the FMH, and most working physicians are members, even though there is no mandatory membership. There are currently 39,000 physicians in the FMH – or about 95% of medical practitioners in Switzerland.

295. Regular membership in the FMH is linked to membership in non-specialist associations. The latter include the cantonal medical associations, the Association of Swiss Assistant and Senior Physicians (*Verband der Schweizerischen Assistenz- und Oberärztinnen und -ärzte*, VSAO), and the Association of Chief Hospital Doctors (*Verein der Leitenden Spitalärzte*, VLSS). All of these associations, as well as the specialist societies, are organized under private law. The FMH recognizes one specialist society in each field, which is permitted to perform important functions within the scope of postgraduate and continuing medical education in its branch of medicine.

296. An important body affiliated with the FMH is the Swiss Institute for Postgraduate and Continuing Medical Education (*Schweizerisches Institut für ärztliche Weiter- und Fortbildung*, SIWF). Its task is to organize accredited postgraduate educational programmes that lead to the acquisition of a Swiss Federal postgraduate degree. The SIWF is thus a central point of contact for postgraduate and continuing medical education. In cooperation with the professional organizations, it develops comprehensive postgraduate and continuing medical education programmes for every field and also issues regulations covering postgraduate and continuing medical education.

II. Professional Codes

297. The violation of professional law in the broader sense ('professional codes') can result in disciplinary actions. However, the disciplinary system can only be fully understood against the backdrop of the important distinction made in Switzerland between state-framed occupational law in the narrower sense and the private rules of professional conduct. The disciplinary authorities' jurisdiction runs along these very lines: while the state (supervisory) authorities enforce state occupational law and punish violations of this law with disciplinary measures, private professional organizations enforce their codes of conduct with respect to members. State law is overseen by state authorities; private association law by the association authorities.

298. State occupational law has already been discussed in the narrower sense. In section A, we will take a closer look at the codes of conduct applicable to Swiss doctors. This will be followed by a discussion of the legal framework and definitions of the disciplinary measures in sections B–D.

A. Codes of Professional Conduct for Swiss Physicians

299. As an association organized under private law, the FMH issues independent regulations – i.e., regulations that are not framed but recognized by the state within the scope of its legal system. These regulations represent binding (association) law for association members (and not only for them). When there are conflicts between state and private professional law, state law takes precedence. The Code of Professional Conduct of the FMH (*Standesordnung der FMH*; hereinafter StaO FMH) embodies the professional ethics of the doctors organized in the association. The cantonal medical associations are permitted to issue supplementary regulations if this is called for in the Code of Professional Conduct.

300. The FMH regulations are supposed to be binding not only for FMH members, but also for all medical practitioners. This is indeed true to the extent that they can be consulted to interpret and concretely define state law when they are an expression of proper professional practice ('state of the art'). Private codes of conduct are usually more stringent than is necessary to ensure proper professional practice in the public's interest. They are aligned with the specific interests of the respective professional group. In such cases, they may be consulted only to a limited degree when there is a need to interpret or concretely define the often abstract professional regulations in the Medical Professions Law or in cantonal law.

301. The FMH's Code of Professional Conduct is divided into the following sections: physicians' conduct toward patients (Articles 4–18), their conduct in public (Articles 19–22), and their conduct toward colleagues (Articles 23–30) and other members of the healthcare system (Articles 31–42). The final chapter of the code deals with the use and enforcement of the regulations (disciplinary actions).

302. The basic provisions stipulate that physicians must practise their profession in a careful and conscientious manner (Article 3, paragraph 1, StaO FMH). Personal integrity and professional competence are prerequisites. Physicians must support quality assurance measures and are obliged to participate in continuing medical education on a regular basis. As far as the social security system goes, they must adhere to the principle of cost-effective medical treatment.

303. According to the principles of treatment (Article 4, StaO FMH), physicians must protect human dignity and their patients' personal rights. They are forbidden to abuse the dependent relationship that can arise from their medical activities. All patients must be treated with the same conscientiousness and care, regardless of their person. Physicians must respect the patients' right to freely choose medical practitioners and, with the exception of emergencies, they themselves are allowed to turn down mandates to provide treatment or information. Physicians must treat patients personally to the extent that this is possible. Furthermore, they are subject to briefing and record-keeping duties and are bound by confidentiality. Medical fees must be appropriate and are based on the applicable fee schedules. The Code of Professional Conduct also treats assisted dying (Article 17, StaO FMH): Passive assisted dying is permitted under certain conditions, but active assisted dying is prohibited. Furthermore, doctors must abide by the medical-ethical guidelines of the Swiss Academy of the Medical Sciences (*Schweizerische Akademie der Medizinischen Wissenschaften*, SAMW). This is also true of other ethically controversial issues, which is why SAMW guidelines are themselves a valid code of conduct providing guidance and assistance in situations in which doctors face difficult decisions.

304. The physicians' conduct in public must be marked by professionalism. This applies not only to their actual appearances in public, which are by all means welcome, but also to advertising. Abuse of titles is inadmissible.

305. Physicians are also obliged to cooperate with one another (Articles 23 et seqq., StaO FMH). If criticism is offered, it must be professional and objective. It is forbidden to 'poach' patients that are being treated by a colleague. An additional professional duty for doctors is that they must support younger colleagues. If possible, disputes should be settled amicably.

306. Physicians are required to practise their professions conscientiously. If they enter into contracts, they must ensure that non-medical third parties are not empowered to give them orders incompatible with this duty. The same applies to doctors who are commissioned by non-medical persons (e.g., insurers, sports associations). Physicians must always be aware of the possibility of conflicts of interest. The medical treatment of athletes is regulated in greater detail in one of the directives in the Code of Professional Conduct (Article 33, StaO FMH). The concrete professional regulations in this field include a ban on issuing false medical certificates, the requirement to take out liability insurance, and a prohibition on referring patients to certain hospitals against payment ('kickbacks'). Medical activities must not be compromised by financial incentive (Article 42, StaO FMH).

307. Doctors must respect the importance of members of other health professions. They must also honour the personal rights of their co-workers and support their training and continuing medical education. Private conduct is considered unworthy if it leaves doctors liable to prosecution or undermines the standing or trustworthiness of the medical profession.

B. Disciplinary Actions due to Violations of Private Codes of Conduct

308. Observance of professional regulations is supervised by the professional commissions of the cantonal medical associations as well as by the VSAO (see Articles 43 et seqq., StaO FMH). These commissions may penalize guilty members with the sanctions listed in the Code of Professional Conduct. The sanctions range from reprimands and penalties to exclusion from the FMH and the withdrawal of FMH degrees (but national continuing medical education degrees are an exception). An additional harsh measure is publication of the disciplinary actions in the medical societies' organs and journals and notification of the responsible authorities. The decisions taken by the cantonal professional commissions may be contested before the FMH's professional commission. In the case of less severe sanctions, only the complaint authority has review powers. If the internal stages of appeal have been exhausted, resort can be made to a state judge (Article 75 ZGB; BGE 118 II 12 [1990]).

309. The proceedings before the professional commission follow FMH regulations and pertinent rules. If these are not suited to finding a solution, the provisions in the Federal Law on Administrative Procedure are applicable (as association law).

310. The proceedings may be suspended or dropped if a case on the same matter is pending before a state authority or court.

C. Disciplinary Actions due to Violations of State Norms

311. As mentioned, the professional commissions do not examine whether state occupational law has been violated. This is a matter for the state supervisory authorities, which are integrated into the cantonal government and in most cases are the cantonal health departments. They are responsible not only for disciplinary actions, but also for the general task of supervising the medical activities that are subject to licensing in the public interest. Consequently, there is no national supervisory authority, nor has supervision been transferred to private medical associations.

312. Occupational law for doctors who practise their profession independently is uniformly regulated at the Federal level in the Medical Professions Law. The same applies to the related disciplinary actions, which are regulated by Federal law exclusively and are binding for the cantons. Article 43 of the Medical Professions Law provides for the following disciplinary measures (starting with the least severe): warnings, reprimands, penalties up to CHF 20,000, a temporary ban on independent professional practice, and – as the most drastic measure – a ban on professional practice for an unlimited period. According to the legal regulations, penalties may be imposed in addition to the ban on professional practice. A ban applies to all of Switzerland (Article 45, Medical Professions Law). Disciplinary actions are recorded in the National Register of the Academic Medical Professions, but they are not made accessible to the public (Articles 52 et seqq., Medical Professions Law).

313. By contrast, physicians who work in the employment of others are subject to cantonal professional regulations. For the professional ban set forth in Article 43 of the Medical Professions Law to be extended to dependent professional practice, there must be a corresponding foundation in cantonal disciplinary law or in professional regulatory law.

314. Disciplinary sanctions may also be imposed on healthcare providers who breach contractual agreements or who violate the cost and quality control regulations in the KVG. Such violations include the refusal to take part in quality assurance measures. In such cases, the competent authority is the (cantonal) social insurance arbitration board, which is usually attached to the cantonal administrative courts or the cantonal insurance courts. In addition to the presiding administrative judge, it consists of one representative of the insurers and one representative of the affected healthcare providers. Possible disciplinary sanctions are defined exclusively in the KVG and range from a warning on reimbursement duties to penalties to the last-resort measure of stripping healthcare providers of their right to charge services to the compulsory health insurance programme. Removing the providers from the health insurance programme only has an '*inter partes*' effect – it concerns only those insurers (or associations) that have applied for their removal.

D. Criminal Sanctions

315. Specialized laws, particularly the KVG and the cantonal health laws, also contain criminal sanctions for violation of concrete state occupational regulations. These sanctions deal primarily with violations of disclosure requirements and compulsory registration. The public has a great interest in effective enforcement of these duties. The violation of private professional codes is not penalized directly. In general, the punitive sanctions consist solely of a penalty. But if the physician's actions are not *lege artis*, general criminal offences naturally apply, including those offences against life and physical integrity (bodily injury and homicide).

E. Principles and Interplay of the Various Sanctions

316. Professional disciplinary measures as well as 'association penalties' ('*Vereinsstrafe*') presuppose fault, whereby negligent breach of duty is sufficient. Intent must not be shown. In contrast to administrative measures and other association penalties, the requirement of demonstrating fault indicates that professional disciplinary measures presuppose personally reproachable conduct. Disciplinary measures and association penalties aim not only to preserve public order but also to punish ('discipline') breaches of professional duty. An important principle in choosing and assessing suitable disciplinary measures is that they be proportionate to the particular breach of duty. The ordered measure must be suitable and necessary in order to achieve the aforementioned goals, and it must also constitute an appropriate punitive action vis-à-vis the concerned party.

317. According to prevailing Swiss legal theory, the various types of sanctions (punitive sanctions, state disciplinary sanctions, association penalties, and administrative measures) can be cumulative. Not applicable here is the criminal-trial principle of *ne bis in idem.* To be heeded in this instance is the principle of proportionality and/or the weighing of interests – i.e., the combination of measures of at least partial punitive character is subject to the principle of proportionality.

318. This also holds for a combination of several disciplinary sanctions. Professional or occupational law does in part contain a clear regulation (e.g., Article 43, paragraph 3, Medical Professions Law; Article 47, StaO FMH). In all other cases, decisions are to be made according to general principles. A combination of disciplinary measures is not prohibited per se, but can be disproportionate in certain individual cases. Disproportionality may not be affirmed if only for the reason that the same incident could possibly provoke disciplinary measures from various authorities. The spirit and purpose of the disciplinary measures should be carefully heeded; for example, according to Article 59 of the KVG, social insurance disciplinary measures primarily protect the insurer, which can also be seen in that the 'exclusion from health insurance' only applies to those health insurance companies that have made application for it. It is not the purpose of Article 59 of the KVG to punish any breach of professional regulations. Professional disciplinary law is applicable here, and cumulatively if necessary.

III. Biomedical Ethics Commission

319. Ethics commissions have no disciplinary powers in Switzerland. Enforcement of professional regulations in the broader sense rests with other authorities. Nevertheless, in this section the most important state and private ethics commissions will be briefly presented.

320. The cantonal ethics commissions are state decision-making bodies that rule on the ethical tenability of research applications in all areas of human medicine. According to Swiss law, approval by the ethics commission is the prerequisite for legal authorization of research projects in the areas of medicinal substances, stem cell research, and transplantations. The cantons are free to expand the authority of their ethics commissions to include other areas. Not every canton needs to install its own ethics commission. For reasons of professionalism and efficiency, cooperation is unavoidable, particularly in smaller cantons.

321. The National Ethics Commission for Human Medicine (NEK), established by the Federal Council in 2001, has a legal mandate to follow the rapid developments in all branches of biomedicine and to adopt an ethical position with regard to the questions arising therefrom. The NEK is not a decision-making body but rather an independent extra-parliamentarian consultative organ, or 'reflective organ'. The commission does not render decisions on concrete research projects; rather, its task is to inform the public, to come up with recommendations for medical practice, and to advise state decision-makers. Nevertheless, the ethical positions assumed by the NEK can carry considerable legal and political weight. In the course of daily legal affairs, consulting and (co-)decision-making flow into each other.

322. Of national importance in pharmaceutical law is the Central Ethics Commission (ZEK). As an organ of the SAMW, which is organized under private law, the ZEK is not a state agency but a private ethics commission. The ZEK takes a stance on medical-ethical questions and develops ethical guidelines to lend assistance to medical practice and biomedical research (SAMW guidelines). Once again, this is a consultative or 'reflective organ'. The importance of the SAMW guidelines can hardly be overestimated. They are referred to in the FMH's Code of Professional Conduct, thus making them professionally binding for doctors. Moreover, the guidelines are used by state ethics commissions and courts. Switzerland's Federal Supreme Court has repeatedly drawn upon the ethical decisions contained in the guidelines. This is controversial, for these are the recommendations of a private organization that discharges no state function.

323. The above is by no means a complete list of all ethics commissions. There are other commissions and organizations, private and state, that deal with ethical issues in biomedicine. Of note are the ethics commissions of cantonal hospitals and universities. Their duties are determined by the authoritative law of the respective organization. They primarily assume an advisory function.

Part II. The Physician: Patient Relationship

Chapter 1. General Description

§1. Rights and Duties of Physicians and Patients

I. Legal Principles

324. There is no federal law in Switzerland governing patients and their rights. The creation of such a law would require a constitutional amendment, since the federal government has only fragmented jurisdiction over the healthcare system. It has, however, made use of this jurisdiction to issue a number of special laws (e.g., the Transplantation Law, the Reproductive Health Law, the Federal Law on Genetic Tests on Humans (GUMG), the Sterilisation Law, the Medication Law, and the Law on Research on Human Beings (HFG)). As *lex specialis*, these laws take precedence over the general legal norms of the federal government and cantons in the respective areas. As regards treatment relationships not subject to special regulation – and in particular that field which is probably the most important in medical practice, namely therapeutic medical treatments – the rights and duties of patients and doctors derive from the general norms of civil, criminal, and public law, in particular from the *Zivilgesetzbuch* (ZGB, Civil Code), the *Obligationenrecht* (OR, Code of Obligations), the *Strafgesetzbuch* (StGB, Penal Code), and the *Bundesverfassung* (BV, Swiss Federal Constitution). To a certain degree, this also applies to treatments that have no direct curative purpose, such as cosmetic surgery. Nevertheless, all the cantons have issued cantonal laws on healthcare and/or patients' rights, drawing on their authority to regulate the healthcare system (see Article 3 and Article 42, BV).

325. Because the Swiss legal system rests on the twin pillars of private and public law, the rights of physicians and patients have different legal foundations depending on whether the legal relationship between the physician and patient is governed by public or private law. Of fundamental importance for treatment relationships under private law are the regulations on the protection of personality rights (Articles 27 and 28, ZGB) and the provisions on simple mandates (Articles 394 et seq., OR), since treatment is normally classified as such. The provisions on the management of an affair without a mandate (Articles 419 et seq., OR) are applicable, in particular, to emergency situations in which the patient is unresponsive and cannot enter into a contract with the doctor. For treatment relationships under public law-,the fundamental rights set forth in the Swiss constitution are of utmost importance, followed by the cantonal laws and ordinances governing healthcare and patients' rights. Furthermore, due to Switzerland's monist tradition, the relevant norms for treatment contained in international legal agreements (primarily the European Convention on Human Rights and the Convention on Biomedicine) are considered directly applicable if their content is sufficiently defined and lucid enough to form the basis of decisions in individual cases ('self-executing norms'). This is considered to be the case if the norm is justiciable, if its content is focused on individual rights and duties, and if it is directed towards those authorities that apply the law (BGE 124 III 90, 91 [1998]). If these requirements are met, private persons may make direct reference to the norms of the international legal agreements without the norm having been adapted to national law. Finally, criminal law provisions can be applied to treatment relationships governed by both private and public law.

326. For some years now, there has been a growing tendency to analyse the private and public law norms relevant to medical law from a comprehensive perspective. This practice has given rise to a coherent cross-sectional branch of law that brings together different legal disciplines and features numerous special laws containing private and public law norms. As a result, patients' rights rest on different legal foundations depending on the underlying legal relationships. Yet despite these different foundations, the content of these rights is largely identical, and they will therefore be described in the following paragraphs based on their content. In individual cases, of course, the different legal foundations have led to differences in the way the rights are framed – to which reference will be made in the appropriate passages.

327. At the start, however, a specific feature of medical treatment under public law must be addressed. Treatment in a public hospital is governed by public law, which means that a patient enters into a so-called special status or institutional relationship ('*Sonderstatus- oder Anstaltsverhältnis*') with the operator of the hospital as opposed to a contract for treatment. This type of relationship differs from contractual relationships under private law in that the rights and duties of patients and doctors are defined by laws and provisions and not negotiated by the two parties. Furthermore, there is no direct legal relationship between the attending physician and the patient. One exception is a patient who is treated by a private physician in a public hospital. In this case, the physician treats the patient in his or her own name and on his or her own account, even though the patient is accommodated at a public hospital. This is known as a split contractual relationship and actually consists of two contracts: a private-law contract for treatment with the attending doctor, and a contract with the public hospital. In practical terms, this relationship exists if a patient is treated in the private ward of a public hospital or if he or she is treated either by a doctor with treatment privileges at a public hospital or the hospital's chief physician.

II. The Rights and Duties in the Doctor-Patient Relationship

A. *The Patient's Right to Self-determination*

328. A central right for competent patients is that of self-determination. It is based on the general protection afforded personality rights (Article 10, BV and Article 28, ZGB) and includes the individual's right to decide independently and of his or her own free will regarding interferences with his or her physical and/or mental integrity. As an expression of respect for the patient's autonomy, the right to self-determination takes precedence over the medical necessity of treatment and basically has priority over the medical-ethical principle of care. This is why a patient capable of giving consent (which means 'competent' in Swiss law) may also refuse procedures necessary to save his or her life, with his or her decision binding. But the doctor must nevertheless attempt to convincingly explain the necessity of treatment to him or her.

329. The law can provide for exceptions to the right of self-determination. These include mentally ill patients who represent an acute danger to themselves or third parties and patients who have contracted certain contagious diseases.

B. *The Right to a Patient Briefing, the Right to Refuse Information, and the Therapeutic Privilege*

330. Swiss law distinguishes between two types of patient briefings. The so-called procedural briefing ('*Eingriffs- oder Selbstbestimmungsaufklärung*') serves to protect the patient's free will and physical integrity – i.e., his or her right to self-determination. A patient can only make a self-determined decision if he or she is informed. The second type of patient briefing, the therapeutic briefing ('*Sicherungs- oder therapeutische Aufklärung*') is intended to promote the success of treatment.

331. As part of the procedural briefing, the physician must inform the patient about the diagnosis, the prognosis, the possible treatments, and all related details including the risks of treatment and expected changes in his or her health (both positive and negative), as well as alternative treatments. The purpose of this briefing is to give the patient the opportunity to make an informed decision in full knowledge of the relevant facts. It enables the patient to make an independent decision and safeguards his or her right to self-determination. On the one hand, the duty to brief the patient is founded on the patient's personality rights (Article 10, BV and Article 28, ZGB), and, on the other, on contract law and the cantonal regulations governed by public law. Without being asked to do so, the doctor must provide all the information the patient needs to appropriately exercise his or her right of self-determination. Nevertheless, according to the decisions of the Swiss Federal Supreme Court, the physician can expect the patient to play an active role in the briefing – i.e., to openly voice any doubts about a certain treatment and to inquire about alternatives.

332. The therapeutic briefing is intended primarily to ensure the success of treatment (see also BGE 116 II 519, 521 [1990]). The physician must properly inform the patient about the treatment, the effects and side effects of prescribed drugs, as well as about everything the patient can do to ensure a successful outcome. Its purpose is to enable the patient to do everything in his or her power to recover. This type of briefing is part of the physician's duty of care.

333. The physician's duty of care and his or her fiduciary duty and duty of accountability (Article 400, paragraph 1, OR) establish an obligation to provide the patient with information on all matters that might be of interest. The doctor must therefore brief the patient on the economic aspects of treatment (BGE 116 II 519, 521 et seq. [1990]), particularly if there are doubts as to whether the costs of treatment will be covered by the health insurance carrier (BGE 119 II 456, 458 et seq. [1993]). In addition, in the current legal literature, the majority view is that the physician's comprehensive fiduciary duty places him or her under an obligation to inform the patient of any errors that the physician or his or her colleagues may have committed during treatment.

334. According to the rulings of the Swiss Federal Supreme Court, the duty to provide information represents the doctor's professional duty, one that obtains irrespective of the legal nature of the underlying treatment relationship (BGE 117 Ib 197, 200 [1991]). The content and scope of the required briefing must be adapted to the patient's needs, to his or her foreknowledge and comprehensive faculty, so that he or she can make an independent and self-determined decision (cf. BGE 117 Ib 197, 204 [1991]).

335. According to Swiss legal scholarship, although this briefing need not take any particular form, the doctor is not permitted to provide information solely in writing on preprinted forms. Nevertheless, he or she may offer a so-called step-by-step briefing ('*Stufenaufkärung*') in which standardized forms or brochures are used to give the patient initial information about the planned procedure and are followed by a talk tailored to the patient's needs. The patient must, however, have the opportunity to ask questions if anything is unclear or if uncertainties remain. With the exception of medical emergencies, this briefing must take place far enough in advance of the inpatient or outpatient treatment for the patient to be able to give careful consideration to the decision and, if need be, to consult with relatives or third parties ('second opinion'). The severity and related risks of the medical procedure should be used to determine the amount of time the patient will be given to think the matter over between the briefing and the procedure.

336. The patient may forgo the briefing either explicitly or through implied behaviour. However, such a renunciation must not be taken lightly and is valid only within certain narrow parameters. For example, with respect to Article 27 of the ZGB, the patient must at least be briefed on the basics of the planned procedure, on its sense, purpose, and necessity, in order that consent can have its justificatory effect. The patient must also be able to revoke his or her decision to forego the briefing at any time (see also Article 27, paragraph 2, ZGB).

337. The patient has the right to be informed as to all the findings regarding his or her health that come to light during diagnostic or therapeutic measures, regardless of whether the doctor was looking for evidence of certain illnesses or whether findings resulted from examinations performed for other purposes ('chance finds'). An exception to the patient's right to information is the so-called therapeutic privilege, which is recognized by the Swiss Federal Supreme Court. According to this principle, because of the duty of care, the physician may (and in fact must) refrain from providing complete and detailed information about a negative diagnosis or prognosis if he or she can expect it to cause such great anxiety in the patient that it would damage the patient's health or seriously endanger his or her recovery (BGE 105 II 284, 288 [1979]; confirmed in BGE 108 II 59, 61 [1982]). Due to the paternalistic focus of the therapeutic privilege, its legality has been sharply criticized by some legal scholars. With an eye towards the patient's right to self-determination, physicians should at any rate exercise restraint in evoking this privilege. If the patient expressly asks for a complete briefing on his or her condition, the physician must meet this request and provide complete and true information – although admittedly in a gentle manner that is in line with the duty of care.

338. The patient may request that he or she not be informed of chance finds (right to ignorance). In other words, either explicitly or through implied behaviour, the patient may show that he or she has no interest in learning about 'secondary findings' that come to light by chance during an examination performed for certain purposes. Nonetheless, the doctor may not treat this renunciation lightly. The *Bundesgesetz über genetische Untersuchungen beim Menschen* (GUMG), or Federal Act on Genetic Tests of Humans, provides for an exception to the patient's right to ignorance: a pregnant woman must be informed immediately of findings if she or her embryo face the immediate, yet avertable, threat of physical danger (Article 18, paragraph 2, GUMG).

C. Treatment According to the Rules of Medical Science, the Duty to Perform

339. In a relationship governed by private law, the patient has no general right to treatment. With the exception of emergency treatment (Article 40 g, MedBG), doctors have the right, based on freedom of contract, to decide for themselves whether they wish to treat a patient or not. In this case, professional ethical requirements are stricter than legal norms. If a treatment relationship is nevertheless established, the doctor is required to treat the patient carefully and in accordance with the rules of medical science. The doctor is therefore bound to observe valid and generally recognized principles of medicine during treatment. In terms of contract law, this duty arises from the respective first paragraphs of Articles 394 and 396 of the Code of Obligations. Nevertheless, the physician does not owe the patient successful treatment or a cure; rather, applying the rules of medical science, he or she is merely required to work towards the goal of the patient's recovery. Moreover, the doctor is prohibited from doing anything that might harm the patient and must act with due care. According to the decisions of the Swiss Federal Supreme Court, however, the duty of care cannot be ultimately defined, but must be based 'on the circumstances of the individual case – namely, on the type of procedure or treatment, the associated risks, the physician's discretion, the time available to him in the individual case, as well as the training and capacity that can be objectively expected of him' (BGE 116 II 519, 521 [1990]). If the doctor is unable to diagnose the illness or treat the patient on his or her own due to lack of the required expertise, bringing in a specialist is then part of the doctor's duty to treat the patient carefully. If the doctor fails to do so, he or she can be charged with negligence for taking on tasks for which he or she is not qualified ('*Übernahmeverschulden*').

340. The patient and doctor may agree on a specific treatment, or they may agree to do without a certain medication. Because of the duty of care and the fiduciary duty under Article 398, paragraph 2, of the Code of Obligations, the physician is responsible for determining the scope of treatment. He or she is under no obligation to meet every patient request. Even if explicitly requested to do so by the patient, the doctor is not required to provide a treatment that violates the rules of medical science or his or her personal convictions. However, in contrast to a request for a specific treatment, the patient's right to refuse treatment is in principle an absolute right. Consequently, if the patient refuses a treatment, the doctor must refrain from treating him or her, even if treatment is crucial to keeping the patient alive. In this case, the patient's right to self-determination takes precedence over the medical principle of providing treatment.

341. Because a special relationship of mutual trust exists between the patient and physician, the physician is ordinarily required to provide treatment personally (see Article 398, paragraph 3, OR). The doctor must inform the patient if he or she cannot guarantee this. Exceptions are possible if the doctor is authorized to assign parts of treatment or treatment in its entirety to a third party, if the doctor is compelled to do so by circumstance, or if it is ordinarily regarded as permissible for the doctor to use a substitute (Article 398, paragraph 3, OR). Supporting tasks may be delegated, but not true medical duties (e.g., providing information).

342. In a relationship governed by public law, the duty to treat a patient may exist on the basis of cantonal law. For emergency patients, this right arises from Article 12 of the Swiss constitution. After consulting with the patient, the doctor in charge makes a decision as to whether to admit (or release) the patient, but there may be exceptions if the hospital has no additional capacity for new patients.

343. The patient has the right to discontinue treatment at any time or to switch doctors, except when treatment is legally stipulated, as is the case for contagious diseases or mandatory treatment within the scope of involuntary commitment. For treatment relationships governed by private law, the right granted to the patient as the 'client' to revoke treatment at any time is laid down in Article 404, paragraph 1, of the Code of Obligations. This right of withdrawal can be exercised in any form and at any time and terminates the contractual relationship with immediate effect starting from the time the patient's decision is made known to the attending doctor. If the patient exercises his or her right of withdrawal at an inopportune moment – making a last-minute decision, for example, not to undergo an operation that is planned for the next day and for which extensive arrangements have already been made – he or she is at most liable for any damages incurred (concerning treatment under private law, see Article 404, paragraph 2, OR). However, this provision may only be invoked to the disadvantage of the patient in cases where an actual violation exists.

D. The Right to Freely Choose a Physician and Hospital

344. In a treatment relationship governed by private law, patients basically have the right to freely choose the doctor they wish to treat them. They may also freely choose specialists. Nevertheless, their contract with the health insurance provider may impose factual restrictions on their choice of doctor. If the costs of treatment are to be borne by their health insurance policy, they must choose a physician who is under contract with that insurer (see Article 41 of the KVG). Since there is *Vertragszwang* in Switzerland – i.e., health insurance providers must in principle enter into a contract with all licensed doctors – this is currently not a problem. Recently, though, there have been discussions on ending these mandatory contractual relations that would allow health insurance providers to terminate contracts with doctors, who in their eyes work uneconomically, and to refuse to conclude a cooperation contract with new doctors in private practice. In 2008, this resulted in a draft bill, which was designed to cut costs in the healthcare system. It was highly controversial since it would have given insurers an extremely powerful position. Not only would it factually have restricted the right to choose doctors freely, it also raised concerns that doctors would postpone or not carry out necessary examinations because of fear of being excluded from a contract. The Federal Assembly rejected the draft bill in 2010. The provisions on restricting licensing for new care providers based on Article 55a of the KVG, which were supposed to be replaced by the provisions allowing for freedom of contract, were modified and brought into force again and are due to expire by 30 June 2019 at the latest.

345. Even now, though, insured parties may voluntarily agree to restrict their right to choose a doctor by, for example, selecting either the family doctor model or a Health Maintenance Organization (HMO) scheme. The latter features a group office in which the doctors are normally employees of the health insurance provider (see Article 41, paragraph 4, and Article 62, KVG). In both these models the patients requiring treatment agree to first consult certain doctors (e.g., the family doctor or the group office) with whom the insurance providers have negotiated favourable rates. If needed, these doctors will send them to specialists. Emergency treatment is seen as an exception. In return, patients can profit from less expensive health insurance premiums, and they can further reduce premiums if they voluntarily restrict their choice of hospitals.

346. Patients with general health insurance may not freely choose physicians in public hospitals, but if the relationship of trust with the physician is impaired, they may ask to be treated by another doctor.

E. Financial Duties

347. The patient's main duty is to pay the stipulated or usual fee (Article 394, paragraph 3, of the Code of Obligations applies to relationships governed by private law). A fee is due even if the doctor and patient have not explicitly discussed the duty to pay remuneration or the amount of the fee before treatment starts. Even if the duty to pay a fee is essentially governed by private law, important questions, specifically the amount of the fee, are regulated by the KVG if the insurance provider is expected to bear the costs of treatment (see Article 44, KVG). For medical services covered by mandatory health insurance, the care provider is not permitted to charge any additional fees or negotiate such with the patient ('fee protection'). The mandatory health insurance that every person residing in Switzerland is required to buy (Article 3, KVG) covers the expense of general services in the event of illness (Article 25, KVG), particular preventative medical measures (Article 26, KVG), birth defects not covered by disability insurance (Article 27, KVG), accidents (Article 28, KVG), maternity care (Article 29, KVG), the legal termination of pregnancy (Article 30, KVG), as well as dental treatment on a very limited scale (Article 31, KVG). The health insurance carriers' duty to pay remuneration is subject to the condition that the services provided are effective, purposeful, and economical (Article 32, KVG).

348. Adult patients are merely responsible for paying a fixed deductible called a 'franchise', which currently amounts to CHF 300 per calendar year (Article 64, paragraph 2a, KVG, and Article 103, paragraph 1, KVV). They are also required to make a co-payment amounting to 10% of the medical expenses that exceed the deductible, capped at CHF 700 per calendar year (Article 64, paragraph 2b, KVG, and Article 103, paragraph 2, KVV). Different deductibles may be negotiated in the contract with the health insurance provider, but they may not exceed CHF 2,500 per year (Article 93, paragraph 1, KVV). For each calendar year, the patient is required to pay medical costs up to the deductible, but in return, he or she can benefit from cheaper premiums.

349. Despite the collective agreements between care providers (doctors, hospitals) and insurers, the patient basically remains the contracting party to the doctor and is liable to the doctor for payment of the fee. The patient may demand reimbursement of the payment from the health insurance company – i.e., a reimbursement less the contractually stipulated deductible and the legally defined 10% co-payment (Article 42, paragraph 1, KVG; Tiers garant system). To better protect the physician's claims, the insurer and the care provider may also agree that the insurer is responsible for payment (Article 42, paragraph 2, KVG; Tiers payant system). In this case, the doctor sends his or her invoice directly to the patient's health insurance carrier, which then makes payment.

350. In addition to the duty to pay the fee, the patient is subject to various ancillary financial duties, in particular the duty to pay the doctor for outlays incurred while performing his or her mandate, plus interest, and the duty to release the patient from any obligations he or she has entered into (Article 402, paragraph 1,

OR). Furthermore, the patient is liable to the doctor for any damages resulting from the mandate if the patient is unable to prove that damages have originated through no fault of his or her own (Article 402, paragraph 1, OR).

351. In treatment relationships governed by public law, the duty to pay remuneration is based on the foundations of public law. Patients who pay expenses directly – i.e., those who are not mandatorily insured or who have additional insurance – are subject to the fees specified in special fee schedules.

F. Fiduciary and Protective Duties

352. The prevailing view in legal doctrine is that the client (patient) and the contractor (doctor) are joined by a special fiduciary relationship from which special fiduciary and protective duties arise. The patient is therefore required to protect the doctor against avertable dangers by informing the doctor of any risks known to him or her, including the existence of a contagious disease that requires special protective measures during examinations.

G. Patient Cooperation

353. Patient cooperation is normally critical for the success of treatment. Cooperation includes taking the prescribed medication (or at least informing the doctor that it has not been taken), keeping doctor's appointments and honestly informing the doctor about all facts important for diagnosis. The underlying legal relationship determines whether the patient has an actual duty to cooperate.

354. In treatment relationships under private law, the prevailing opinion in legal literature is that patient cooperation is not a genuine contractual duty but merely an obligation. If the patient violates his or her obligation to cooperate, the patient may, under certain circumstances, forfeit legal claims against the doctor. If, for example, the patient sues the doctor for compensation, the doctor may invoke the patient's lack of cooperation (e.g., dishonest or incomplete information about facts essential for treatment). But since this is not a matter of a real contractual duty, the patient is not liable to the doctor for damages.

355. A different situation presents itself if treatment occurs in a public hospital and is subject to public law. Due to the special status relationship established, the cantons may demand more extensive patient cooperation than would be possible in treatment under private law. Cooperation often includes the duty to provide truthful information, to follow hospital regulations, to show consideration to other patients, and to obey staff instructions. Nevertheless, these duties are always circumscribed by the patient's right to self-determination. Nor can the patient be forced to take medication or to follow therapeutic instructions in treatments governed by public law, except in cases of sanctioned forced treatment.

§2. INFORMED CONSENT

356. According to the prevailing view in legal doctrine and the constant decisions of the Swiss Federal Supreme Court, under public, civil, and criminal law, all medical interventions – even those performed for therapeutic purposes – constitute a violation of the patient's physical and, possibly, mental integrity. As such they are in principle unlawful and must be justified by the patient's consent (BGE 127 I 6, 17 [2001]; BGE 124 IV 258, 260 [1998]; BGE 117 Ib 197, 201 [1991]). The patient's physical and mental integrity is protected in a number of ways: by the right to life and personal liberty, set forth in the constitution (Article 10, BV); by personality rights in civil law (Article 28, ZGB); and by the offence of bodily injury in criminal law (Articles 111 et seq., StGB). In keeping with the principle of *volenti non fit iniuria*, the illegality of the violation of physical integrity can ordinarily only be neutralized by the consent of the patient or, if the patient is incompetent, by the consent of his or her legal representative. Permissible forced treatment is an exception. In the view of the Swiss Federal Supreme Court, the requirement of consent safeguards the patient's right to self-determination and his or her physical integrity (see BGE 117 IB 197, 200 et seq. [1991]). According to this view, both legally protected rights are inextricably linked.

357. The patient may revoke consent at any time (Article 27, paragraph 2, ZGB). The validity of this consent is subject to strict requirements because of its special function in medical law as a means of safeguarding the patient's right to self-determination. First of all, patients may give consent only if they have the intellectual and volitional faculties necessary to make a decision about the planned treatment and to act in keeping with this decision, that is, to defend it against possible opposition. Hence, according to Swiss law, the ability to give consent presupposes competence, which is defined as the ability to act rationally (see Article 16, ZGB). By law, competence is assumed to exist except in cases where the patient is a minor or suffers from mental disease, mental deficiency, intoxication, or similar conditions in which the assumption of competence is invalidated. Competence must always be assessed in relation to a specific point in time and concrete circumstances. It may not be abstractly confirmed or negated ('relativity of competence'). Concerning medical decisions, a patient is considered to be competent if he or she understands the advantages, disadvantages, and possible risks of the planned medical procedure as well as its significance for his or her life and the consequences that may arise from forgoing treatment. In addition, the patient must be able to make a decision and act in accordance with this decision – i.e., he or she must, to a certain extent, be able to withstand external influences.

358. Furthermore, consent must reflect the patient's free will. Because a person can exercise free will only if he or she has sufficient information about the facts of the case, a legally valid briefing is a requirement for valid consent. This briefing is therefore essential for the person consenting to the medical procedure.

359. In cases of patients without legal capacity, the applicable provisions in private law are those governing agency without authority (Articles 419 et seq. OR) and legal representation with regard to medical procedures (Articles 377 et seq. ZGB). If, due to injuries or illness, the patient lost legal capacity, the doctor must consult the advance healthcare directive (*Patientenverfügung*, living will, Article 377, paragraph 1, Article 370 ZGB). The doctor must comply with the patients advance directive unless it violates statutory regulations or there is reasonable doubt that it is based on the patient's free will or still corresponds to his or her presumed will (Article 372, paragraph 2, ZGB). An advance directive must fulfil the following conditions to be valid: It must be composed in writing, dated, and signed (Article 371, paragraph 1, ZGB). At the time of its being drawn up, the author must be competent – however, a person need not have attained his or her majority, as the drawing up of an advance directive impinges upon strictly personal rights (Article 19c, ZGB, particularly the right to self-determination over the integrity of one's own body). Furthermore, the medical measure concerned must be indicated. If these prerequisites are fulfilled, an advance directive has in principle the same binding force as an actual declaration of consent (Article 372, paragraph 2, ZGB; *Botschaft Erwachsenenschutz*, 7033), except if the advance directive violates statutory regulations or there is reasonable doubt that it is based on the patient's free will or still corresponds to his or her presumed will (Article 372, paragraph 2, ZGB). The reasons for any departures from the advance directive must be explained by the physician in the patient's medical records (Article 372, paragraph 3, ZGB). In an advance directive, a person may also designate another person who is authorized to discuss the medical procedures with the attending doctor and decide on the patient's behalf. Moreover, it is possible to issue instructions to this person (Article 370, paragraph 2, ZGB). One may furthermore issue alternative instructions for the event that the designated person is not suitable for the tasks, does not accept the mandate, or terminates the mandate (Article 370, paragraph 3, ZGB).

360. The problem with an advance directive is that future scenarios are generally hard to anticipate. Advance directives are often laid down without any prior expert counselling about the rejected or desired medical measures. They are composed far in advance of the patient's medical condition, and are not tailored to meet an individual patient's needs but are rather standardized preprinted documents that merely demand a patient's signature.

361. The advance directive can be revoked any time in writing (must be dated and signed), by destroying the document or by drawing up a new advance directive (Article 371, paragraph 3, ZGB and Article 362, ZGB). Legal scholarship is in disagreement of whether a posterior oral statement constitutes a revocation of an advance directive or is merely a sign for a change in the patient's presumed will. With regard to Article 27 of the ZGB, the former appears to apply. No person may surrender his or her freedom or restrict the use of it to a degree which violates the law or public morals.

362. Any person closely related to the patient may contact the adult protection authority and claim that the patient's provisions are not being complied with, the interests of the patient are being endangered or no longer safeguarded,; or the advance directive is not based on the patient's free will (Article 373, paragraph 1,

ZGB). The term 'person closely related to the patient' refers e.g., to relatives, friends, caregivers, and doctors. The emotional relationship is hereby decisive.

363. If the patient has not given instructions concerning the treatment in an advance directive, or for any reason the advance directive is invalid, the attending doctor must plan the required treatment in consultation with the person entitled to act as legal representative of the patient (Article 377, paragraph 1, Article 378 ZGB). The legal representative of the patient has to decide according to the patient's presumed will (as, e.g., expressed in the patient's past statements or values) and to his interests. The presumed will is a normative concept. It is determined by what the patient would decide if he or she was competent. Relatives, the family doctor, and other persons to whom the patient relates closely may provide information about his or her past statements, past decisions, and values. While the presumed clearly has a subjective dimension, the patient's interests are defined exclusively by objective medical criteria. If treatment is both medically indicated and necessary, it may be ordinarily assumed that it is in conformity with the patient's presumed will and interests unless there is a reason to believe otherwise (e.g., patient's past statements). The medical indication limits the power of representation. The legal representative cannot validly consent to a treatment which is not medically indicated. The ZGB does not specify what takes priority in case of contradiction between the presumed will of the patient and his or her objective interests.

364. If possible, the patient should also be involved in the decision-making (Article 377, paragraph 3, ZGB). The extent of involvement depends on his or her capability to express own wishes and preferences. Legal scholarship holds the view that in cases in which incompetence of the patient constitutes only a temporary state, and the decision concerning the medical treatment can be postponed without detriment until the patient regains the power of judgment, the provisions concerning legal representation (Articles 377 et seq. ZGB) should not apply.

365. Article 378 of the ZGB regulates conclusively who is entitled to represent the incompetent person and to grant or refuse consent to measures of treatment. The following statutory predefined order of priority of representatives is legally binding: a person appointed in an advance care directive (*Patientenverfügung* or *Vorsorgeauftrag*) (no. 1); a representative deputy (*Beistand/Beiständin*) with a right to act as a legal representative with regard to medical procedures (no. 2); any person who as a spouse or registered partner cohabits with the incompetent patient or who regularly and personally provides him or her with support (no. 3); any person who cohabits with the incompetent patient or who regularly and personally provides him or her with support (no. 4); offspring who regularly and personally provide the incompetent patient with support (no. 5); the parents, if they regularly and personally provide the incompetent patient with support (no. 6); and siblings, if they regularly and personally provide the incompetent patient with support (no. 7).

366. According to Article 381, paragraph 1, of the ZGB the adult protection authority (*Erwachsenenschutzbehörde*) establishes a representative deputyship

(*Vertretungsbeistandschaft*) if there is no representative available or the representative does not wish to exercise the right to act. If it is unclear who has a right to act as representative, or the persons with a right to act as representatives are unable to agree, the adult protection authority appoints a representative or establishes a representative deputyship (Article 381, paragraph 2, ZGB). The adult protection authority acts thereby at the request of the doctor or of another closely with the patient associated person or ex officio (Article 381, paragraph 3, ZGB). The doctor or another closely with the patient associated person can advise the adult protection authority if he or she is of the opinion that a certain measurement is not compatible with the patient's presumed will and interests (Article 381, paragraph 2 c, ZGB).

367. In urgent cases, where there is no time to consult the patient's provisions or his or her legal representative, or to await a decision of the adult protection authority without detriment to the patient's conditions, the doctor may carry out medical procedures according to the presumed will and interests of the patient (Article 379 ZGB).

§3. Privacy

368. Patients have an absolute right to the protection of their privacy, which of course includes medical data. In treatment relationships governed by private law, medical data fall under the protection offered personality rights in Article 28 of the ZGB. In relationships governed by public law, medical data are protected by the personal liberties enumerated in Article 10 of the Swiss Federal Constitution and are also safeguarded by cantonal regulations. The doctor's duty to maintain strict confidentiality also derives from the private-law contractual relationship between doctor and patient. At issue in this private-law relationship are the fiduciary duty that exists by law (Article 398, paragraph 2, OR). It is therefore unnecessary for the physician and patient to enter into an explicit confidentiality agreement. From the perspective of private law, the duty of confidentiality covers all of the information that the doctor receives from the patient, the patient's relatives, or third parties, as well as all of the information that becomes known to the doctor through the diagnostic measures he or she performs. In short, it touches upon everything that the doctor learns within the scope of treatment, provided the patient has a subjective interest in its confidentiality. This duty of confidentiality also applies to dealings with the patient's spouse, partner, or relatives. A competent patient may authorize the doctor to provide information about the state of his or her health to relatives or certain third parties. Some cantonal regulations allow the doctor to assume he or she has consent from the patient to inform relatives. If the patient is incompetent due, for example, to unconsciousness, the doctor must inform the patient's relatives or other people close to the patient so that the doctor may receive information from them on the patient's presumed desires.

§4. CONFIDENTIALITY

369. Medical confidentiality derives from the personality rights granted in public and private law and is additionally protected under criminal law. Under Article 321 of the StGB, doctors, dentists, pharmacists, midwives, and their auxiliaries can be punished with up to three years' imprisonment or a fine if they deliberately disclose the confidential information with which they have been entrusted due to their professions or that they have learned while performing their duties. Students in these disciplines are also subject to professional confidentiality. That said, criminal prosecution is only initiated if charges are filed, and negligence is not subject to punishment.

370. Actions are not punishable if the confidential information is disclosed because of consent from an authorized person or written approval from either the responsible authority or a supervisory body. Other exceptions include the possible duty to inform authorities and the duty to appear in court as a witness. An additional justification for disregarding the professional duty of confidentiality is the patient's presumed consent, particularly if the patient is unconscious at the start of treatment and the doctor must make a decision, based on the available evidence, as to whether he or she is allowed to inform relatives. As a rule, the doctor may assume in such situations that he or she has permission to notify the patient's closest relatives and brief them about the patient's health.

371. The purpose of this provision of criminal law is to ensure that the public has trust in the members of the professions named in the law and to protect the privacy of the affected parties. Only the people and their auxiliaries mentioned in the law can be considered offenders. Auxiliaries are defined as all those people who support, in any way, the person sworn to confidentiality and who, due to this activity, are also privy to the confidential information themselves. They include secretaries, accountants, trainees, nursing staff, assistants, and laboratory employees.

372. In the criminal provision, confidential information is defined as 'every fact that is known to a limited group of people only and that the affected party has a legitimate interest in keeping confidential'. Such facts include the patient's identity and the information that he or she is being treated by a doctor. The confidential information must become known to the doctors or their auxiliaries when they practise their professions, either because the patient has confided it to the doctor or the doctor has learned it from either a third party (e.g., a specialist) or through diagnostic measures. A person discloses this information if he or she deliberately shares it with a third party, or if a person accepts the possibility of a third party taking notice of it – perhaps by negligently leaving medical records lying around. It is immaterial whether the third parties are themselves bound by confidentiality. The doctor is therefore forbidden to discuss the case with other experts without the patient's authorization. Nevertheless, discussions with other team members treating the patient do not violate the duty of confidentiality.

373. When the patient is a minor or incapacitated, it must be decided whether he or she is competent. In principle, competent patients may decide for themselves whether information about their health may be passed on to parents or guardians. In the case of incompetent patients, however, the parents or guardians are considered the 'owners' of the information. Since they are entitled to give consent, they must be informed.

374. Doctors who work in an official capacity (e.g., cantonal doctors, court experts, employees of institutes of medical law) are subject to Article 320 of the StGB. This provision protects the confidential information to which holders of official positions are privy.

§5. Complaints

375. The explanations about doctors' liability in Part II, Chapter 1, §1.II can be consulted for suits based on improper patient briefing or malpractice in a treatment relationship.

§6. Access to Medical Records

I. The Duty to Keep Medical Records

376. In a treatment relationship governed by private law, the physician's duty to keep medical records is based on both the patient's personality rights (Article 28, ZGB) and on contractual law, specifically on the commissioned agent's duty of accountability (Article 400, OR). In a treatment relationship governed by public law, the duty to keep medical records derives not only from the physician's duty of care and the fundamental right of personal liberty (Article 10, paragraph 2, BV), but also from Article 8 of the ECHR, and from cantonal laws and ordinances. An absence of medical records or incomplete records constitutes a breach of contract and, under public law, a violation of the physician's duty of care.

II. Content of Medical Records

377. A patient's medical records include all the documents that the physician has collected in the course of treatment or that were delivered to him by others (hospitals, other physicians): surgical reports, X-rays, laboratory findings, medical expert reports, the content of the patient's medical history, past treatments, prescribed medications, differential diagnoses, and so forth. The medical records must also indicate whether and how the patient was briefed. Records created by physicians in private practice and by private hospitals fall under the regulations of the *Datenschutzgesetz* (DSG), or Data Privacy Law, but this law does not apply to medical records created in public cantonal hospitals, which are subject to the DSGs of the respective canton.

III. Inspection of Medical Records

378. Patients have the right to inspect their medical records and to have copies made. From the perspective of private law, this right is based on the patient's personality rights (Article 28, ZGB) and the provisions of contract law (Article 400, paragraph 1, OR). It is also a feature of public law treatment relationships, where it results from Article 8 of the ECHR, the fundamental right of personal freedom (Article 10, BV), the principle of equality before the law (Article 8, BV), and the due process of law (Article 29, paragraph 2, BV). Moreover, it is explicitly mentioned in numerous cantonal laws. The right to access information pertains to all aspects of a patient's medical history, including the handwritten notes taken by the physician insofar as they concern the patient's diagnosis, treatment, and care, and are thus part of the entire medical history. According to the prevailing opinion among legal scholars, though, the physician is not required to give the patient the original medical records, with the exception of X-rays and other documents created at the request of the patient under private law. These are the patient's property and must be handed over to the patient on demand.

IV. Medical Records and Data Security

379. The provisions of the DSG regulate private collections of data. This law was enacted to protect the personality and fundamental rights of the people about whom the information is collected (Article 1, DSG). Its field of application includes the processing of personal data by private persons (natural persons and legal entities) and by federal bodies (Article 2, paragraph 1, DSG). The DSG is therefore applicable to data pools compiled by independently practicing doctors and private hospitals as well as to data collected by insurance companies and health insurance providers. Public hospitals (except those operated by the federal government) are subject to cantonal DSGs. The DSG regards data on personal health – such as diagnoses, prescriptions, X-rays, and medical records – as especially worthy of protection (Article 3c, no. 2, DSG). The DSG grants the patient a comprehensive and far-reaching right to access information collected about him or her (Article 8, DSG). As a result, all patients may ask their physicians for information about their medical history without having to justify the request. These records must normally be provided in writing, in the form of a printout or a photocopy, free of charge. As a consequence, patients need not content themselves with viewing the records in the doctor's office. The doctor's duty to provide information basically covers all information kept about the patient. However, the DSG does not apply to personal data that a person stores solely for personal use and does not disclose to third parties (Article 2, paragraph 2a, DSG). This means that the private notes taken by a doctor solely for his or her personal use do not come under the duty to provide information (see Article 2, paragraph 2a, DSG). This provision must nevertheless be interpreted restrictively in connection with the patient's right to access medical records, and it must not be misused in an attempt to evade such rights. If the medical records include remarks of a personal nature about the patient but these remarks are accessible to all the other people involved in treating the patient (e.g., the nursing staff), they are not regarded as the doctor's personal notes in the sense of the above-mentioned provision.

380. According to Article 5, paragraph 2, of the DSG, everybody may demand that incorrect data collected about them be rectified. If medical records contain untrue information about the patient, the patient may therefore demand that the information be corrected or destroyed or that its disclosure to third parties be blocked (Article 15, paragraph 1, DSG). At the very least, the patient may demand that a relevant note be made in the records (Article 15, paragraph 2, DSG).

V. Developments

381. In 2007, the Swiss Federal Council launched the e-health project to provide easier access to patients' medical records. Within the scope of the strategy 'Health 2020' (*Gesundheit 2020*), the Council's aim is to successively set up a system for the electronic management of these records. It will feature quality-assured online information and access to medical records. The draft bill concerning the implementation of an electronic management of patients' medical records is currently pending in parliament.

Chapter 2. The Physician-Patient Relationship in Specific Terms

§1. Patients Who Are Minors

382. According to Swiss law, people reach the age of majority at 18 (Article 14, ZGB). Minors are basically incapable of action – i.e., their actions cannot form the basis of rights or duties (Articles 12, 13, ZGB). Exceptions exist in the field of so-called strictly personal rights (*'höchstpersönliche Rechte'*), which are subject to special regulations and protections. These rights are accorded to individuals on the basis of their personality and are inextricably linked to personality. As the law does not specify which rights are included among these strictly personal rights, they must be decided on a case-by-case basis, and an extensive casuistry has grown up around the issue over the years. Under Article 19c, paragraph 1, of the ZGB, competent minors and incapacitated persons may exercise the rights granted to them on the basis of their personality without their legal representative's consent, with the exception of situations in which a legal statute explicitly specifies a fixed minimum age or provides for joint decision-making power on the part of the legal representative. Because strictly personal rights are basically incompatible with the concept of agency, some legal scholars consider the parents' authority to represent children to be invalid if the children are competent. According to this view, a competent minor must make decisions on strictly personal rights him- or herself. But other legal scholars maintain that parents may also act as representatives for their competent children in matters involving strictly personal rights as long as the children do not explicitly reject this.

383. Strictly personal rights include the right to self-determination over physical integrity and, consequently, the right to consent to medical procedures. Competent minors may therefore exercise strictly personal rights independently and without the approval of their legal representatives (ordinarily their parents). Furthermore, they may validly give their informed consent to medical procedures, provided that special laws do not link their right to give consent to a certain minimum age or require the cumulative consent of parents or guardians (as is the case with the Transplantation Law and the Sterilisation Law). The attending physician is responsible for deciding whether a patient is competent. On the one hand, legal capacity presupposes that the minor is capable of roughly understanding his or her situation, the possible treatments, the risks and the consequences of non-treatment, and that the patient is also able to make an independent decision; on the other hand, it presupposes that the minor can act in accordance with this decision. Nevertheless, competence must not be subject to exaggerated demands. It is impermissible, in particular, to declare a person incompetent on the grounds that the decision he or she makes is objectively irrational. On the other hand, special attention must be paid to whether decisions are made independently. The only decisions to meet this criterion are those that are truly made on the basis of the patient's free will and independent of external influences. Exaggerated fear of certain types of treatment can be regarded as grounds for overruling a rejection of such treatments due to a lack of competence. Moreover, there is a general consensus that a competent minor may enter into a contract for treatment independently and without the consent of his or her legal representative if the treatment in question is common and cost efficient or the costs are covered by the health insurance provider (Article 305 and Articles 19 et seq., ZGB) unless the applicable statute requires a certain age limit or a cumulative consent of the legal representative (e.g., Article 12 a *Transplantationsgesetz* or Article 3 *Sterilizationsgesetz*; cf. above regarding consent of minors).

384. In the case of incompetent underage patients, the legal representative is responsible for determining the medical procedures and entering into a contract for treatment (Article 305 and Article 19c, paragraph 2, ZGB). As a rule, parents have custody of their children and are their legal representatives (Articles 296 et seq. and Article 304, paragraphs 1, ZGB). In exceptional cases, the legal representative may be the deputy (*Beistand/Beiständin*, Article 308, paragraph 2, ZGB) or the guardian (*Vormund*, Article 311, paragraph 2, and Article 327c, paragraph 1, ZGB). A guardian is to be appointed when parental responsibility is withdrawn from both parents (Article 311, paragraph 2, ZGB), whereas a deputyship can be established while the parents or one of the parents maintain parental responsibility. When making decisions, parents, deputies, or guardians have to give paramount consideration to the child's welfare (Article 296, Article 301, paragraph 1, ZGB and Article 307, paragraphs 1 and 2, ZGB). They may therefore only validly consent to medical treatments that are in the child's best interest. Whether a certain treatment is in the child's best interest is objectively determined by whether the treatment is necessary based on the recognized principles of medical science. Nevertheless, the child's welfare is not limited to purely physical welfare and also includes mental, social, and, to a certain extent, even cultural dimensions. If the child's welfare can, in good faith, be assessed in different ways, the parents have the authority to determine which treatment best ensures the child's welfare. Nevertheless, if the parents refuse to consent to a medically necessary treatment that cannot be postponed and is absolutely imperative for the child's objective welfare, the attending physicians may request the child protection authority or the deputy appointed by it (Articles 307 et seq., ZGB) to provide the necessary consent. If, in an emergency, no time remains to consult the child protection authority, the physicians must carry out the medically necessary treatment, even in defiance of the parents' wishes, since the parents enjoy no representative authority beyond the bounds of the child's welfare.

385. The parents may not consent to medical treatments that affect absolute, strictly personal rights (Article 19c, paragraph 2, ZGB). These are rights that are so closely linked to the personality of the holder as to make representative authority appear absolutely inadmissible. However, medically indicated and necessary procedures that cannot be postponed and are performed for curative, diagnostic, or preventive purposes (e.g., vaccinations) do not fall under this category. To some extent, special laws also limit the legal representative's authority to consent to medical procedures for incompetent minors. Such regulations can be found, for example, in the Sterilisation Law, the Transplantation Law, the Medication Law, and the GUMG.

386. The personality rights of competent minors encompass also the claim for confidentiality. Disclosure of medical information to parents of the minor requires the consent of the competent minor (Article 28, paragraph 2, ZGB and Article 321,

StGB). While an implied consent is sufficient in principle, it must be examined with due care whether it can be concluded from a particular behaviour. Under certain circumstances, the right to confidentiality can be restricted, e.g., when the minor intends to commit suicide. Usually, the doctor is nevertheless required to obtain the authorization from the responsible authority – typically the Federal Health Office. Furthermore, the disclosure of minor's medical information does not constitute a breach of professional confidentiality obligation when a relevant statute provides for a right or an obligation to report to an authority (Article 321, paragraph 3, StGB and, e.g., Article 364 StGB, where an offence has been committed against a minor).

§2. The Mental Patient

I. General Principles

387. People suffering from mental illness are basically subject to the same provisions as those who have contracted physical illnesses. Once again, the decisive question is whether the patient is competent. Competence may not be generally negated for the mentally ill. If a patient is competent, he essentially decides for himself whether a possible treatment is permissible. Nevertheless, the principle of the relative nature of competence has a special significance in the context of psychiatric treatment. Competence is factually and temporally relative – i.e., it must be judged in relation to a concrete time and concrete circumstances. As a consequence, it must be reassessed at regular intervals, particularly in the case of mental illnesses that progress in sudden and acute phases.

388. A person without power of judgment cannot validly consent to a treatment. The ZGB draws a distinction between rules concerning incompetent persons with regard to medical procedures in general (Articles 377 et seq. ZGB, see above Part II, Chapter 1, §2) and rules concerning incompetent patients with a mental disorder who are treated in a psychiatric clinic (Article 380 and Articles 426 et seq. ZGB). If an incompetent patient is being treated in a psychiatric clinic, the provisions governing care-related (involuntary) hospitalization (*Die fürsorgerische Unterbringung*) apply as a rule. These rules limitation powers for relatives reacted in contrast to the provisions on representation of incompetent persons with regard to medical procedures in general. The legislator justifies the limitation of the power of representation with the protection of mentally ill patients against psychiatric treatment at the hands of relatives.

II. Care-Related Hospitalization and Compulsory Treatment

A. Care-Related Hospitalization

389. The care-related hospitalization is regulated in Articles 426 et seq. of the ZGB. These federal law provisions define the preconditions under which the involuntary hospitalization in an appropriate institution is legitimate. The care-related hospitalization is an involuntary measure, which deprives the patient of his or her freedom. As a measure for the purpose of adult protection, it addresses competent and incompetent patients likewise. As an act of sovereignty it is bound by constitutional rights. According to the Swiss Federal Constitution violations of constitutional rights must have a foundation in formal law, be justified by public interest or the need to protect the basic rights of a third party, be proportionate and must not violate the core content of fundamental rights (Article 36, BV). With the adoption of Articles 426 et seq. of the ZGB not only the federal foundation in formal law was established, but also the relevant criteria for weighing the interests in accordance with Article 36 of the Swiss Federal Constitution were specified.

B. Preconditions for Care-Related Hospitalization and Discharge

390. On the one hand, care-related hospitalization is a last resort in the context of child and adult protection measures; on the other hand, it must be ordered if the requirements of the provisions governing it are met. According to Article 426, paragraph 1, of the ZGB a person suffering from a mental disorder or mental disability or serious neglect may be committed to an appropriate institution if the required treatment or care cannot be provided otherwise.

391. Within the scope of the provisions on care-related hospitalization, mental disorders are clinical psychoses and psychopathies, dementia and all forms of addiction recognized by psychiatry (*Botschaft Erwachsenenschutz*, 7043). A mental disability is a congenital impairment, or an impairment following a disease or an accident, of cognitive functioning with varying degrees of severity. A serious neglect is described as a condition which is no more compatible with human dignity of the concerned person and therefore must be treated (*Botschaft Erwachsenenschutz*, 6062).

392. A mental disorder or mental disability or serious neglect must result in a need for treatment or care which cannot be provided otherwise than by means of care-related hospitalization (e.g., outpatient measures, home care). Care-related hospitalization is only legitimate if an appropriate institution for the specific purpose of treatment and care exists and is available respectively.

393. When interests are weighed, the burden that the patient places on family members and third parties and their protection must be taken into account (Article 426, paragraph 2, ZGB). While there is an agreement among scholars that the protection of third parties as such cannot justify the care-related hospitalization, a serious risk to the life or the physical integrity of others can warrant a detention of a person admitted voluntarily to a psychiatric clinic (Article 427, paragraph 1, no. 2, ZGB). The serious risk must have its cause in a mental disorder. If this is not the case, police measures which serve the public interest and are intended to protect the safety of third parties must be taken into consideration.

394. Compulsory admission to a psychiatric clinic must further comply with the principles of proportionality and may therefore only be ordered if the person in question cannot be provided with the necessary help by other, less extreme measure.

395. Furthermore, all involuntarily hospitalized persons may appoint a trusted third party to support them during hospitalization and the related procedures (Article 432, ZGB). The trusted third party can access the patient's medical records with his or her consent, visit the patient anytime and he or she must be consulted when drawing up the written treatment plan (Article 433, paragraph 1, ZGB). In case of compulsory treatment, the person concerned and his or her trusted third party must be given written notice (Article 434, paragraph 2, ZGB). The trusted person is also authorized to appeal to the court (Article 439, ZGB and Article 450, paragraph 2, no. 2 ZGB). The right to appoint a trusted third party is an absolute, strictly personal right (Article 19c, paragraph 2, ZGB). Hence, only the patient him- or herself can appoint the trusted person.

396. Moreover, it is legitimate to admit a person to an appropriate institution for a psychiatric assessment, if the assessment is essential and cannot be carried out on an outpatient basis (Article 449, paragraph 1, ZGB). However, in these cases a compulsory treatment is inadmissible. The provisions regarding the procedure for care-related hospitalization apply *mutatis mutandis* (Article 449, paragraph 2, ZGB).

397. As soon as the requirements for hospitalization are no longer fulfilled, the patient must be discharged (Article 426, paragraph 3, ZGB). The patient or a closely related person may request his or her discharge at any time. The request is not subject to any particular form and must not supply grounds for the discharge. The required power of judgment will be usually assumed. A decision about the request must be made immediately (Article 426, paragraph 4, ZGB), and its rejection can be challenged before a court (Article 439, paragraph 1, no. 3 ZGB).

398. If in case of discharge there is a risk that the medical condition will recur, the attending doctor shall attempt to agree with the patient on principles for treatment in the event that the patient is committed to the institution again (Article 436, paragraph 1, ZGB). The pre-discharge interview must be documented (Article 436, paragraph 2, ZGB).

399. The follow-up care falls within the jurisdiction of the cantons (Article 437, paragraph 1, ZGB). They may provide for outpatient measures (Article 437, paragraph 2, ZGB). The follow-up care encompasses measures which are organized by the institution or the adult protection authority in consultation with the patient. They are voluntary and serve the purpose of avoiding that the person concerned is committed to the institution again, e.g., visiting day or night clinic, moving to a residential institution or establishing assistance for daily life. The follow-up care envisages support and counselling of the person and is not a medical treatment. Outpatient measures are measures that are ordered by a responsible authority in order to avoid a repeated hospitalization, e.g., the obligation to report to an authority or department periodically, to take medically indicated medication under the supervision of home care staff or to use depot injection. It is contested whether medication prescribed within the scope of outpatient measures can be administered by physical force. According to Swiss Federal Supreme Court decisions, an obligation to undergo medical treatment after discharge from the care-related hospitalization constitutes a compulsory treatment, which in the view of the fact that it severely interferes with constitutional rights requires taking the proportionality principle into account. A thorough and comprehensive weighing of interests is therefore necessary.

C. *Jurisdiction and Proceedings*

400. The adult protection authority is responsible for prescribing involuntary hospitalization and for discharging the patient (Article 428, paragraph 1, ZGB). In specific cases, it may delegate the responsibility for discharging the patient to the institution where he or she is hospitalized (Article 428, paragraph 1, ZGB). The jurisdiction is with the adult protection authority at the place of residence of the person concerned (Article 442, paragraph 1, ZGB). In urgent cases, the authority where the person concerned is actually residing has jurisdiction (Article 442, paragraph 2, ZGB). As a rule, the person concerned must be heard by the adult protection authority as a panel (Article 447, paragraph 2, ZGB). In exceptional cases, the hearing can be delegated to a sole member of the authority, e.g., if there is a risk in delay, out of consideration for the mental health of the person concerned or for reasons of procedural economy. On rare occasions, the hearing can be delegated to an expert outside the authority. In case of hospitalization on grounds of a mental disorder, the adult protection authority must base its decision on an expert opinion, unless the required expertise is given with the authority itself.

401. The adult protection authority must review on a regular basis whether the requirements for hospitalization are still being met and whether the institution is still appropriate, for the first not later than six months after hospitalization (Article 431 ZGB).

402. The cantons may grant eligible doctors the authority to hospitalize patients for a maximum of six weeks (Article 429, ZGB). The responsibility to discharge patients who were hospitalized by a doctor lies with the institution (Article 429, paragraph 3, ZGB). The hospitalization may not continue beyond the specified period of time, unless an enforceable hospitalization order from the adult protection authority applies (Article 429, paragraph 2, ZGB). Usually, the adult protection authority's decision on hospitalization is enforceable immediately (cf. Article 450e, paragraph 2, ZGB).

403. In case of admission by a doctor, specific procedural provisions apply. According to Article 430, paragraph 1, of the ZGB, the doctor must examine and hear the patient in person. The hospitalization order must contain at least the following information: the place and date of the examination; the name of the doctor; the diagnosis, the reason, and the purpose of hospitalization; instructions on the rights of appeal (Article 430, paragraph 2, ZGB). A copy of the hospitalization order must be given to the patient, and a further copy must be given to the institution on the patient's admission (Article 430, paragraph 4, ZGB). If possible, the doctor shall also notify a person closely related to the patient (Article 430, paragraph 5, ZGB). However, the patient's personality rights must be respected. Therefore, no third person can be informed against the patient's will.

404. The doctor's decision on hospitalization is usually also immediately enforceable. An appeal does not have suspensive effect unless the doctor or the competent court orders otherwise (Article 430, paragraph 3, ZGB).

D. Detention of Persons Admitted Voluntarily

405. Most patients are voluntarily admitted to psychiatric clinics and are not subject to the provisions on care-related hospitalization. However, voluntariness presupposes the power of judgment. If a patient is incompetent, a care-related hospitalization is in turn necessary.

406. Moreover, in case of a voluntary admission, the patient can decide to leave the clinic before the treatment is completed. The patient may be detained against his or her will by the institution's medical management for a maximum of three days if he or she is suffering from a mental disorder and is a risk to his or her own life or physical integrity, or if he or she poses a serious risk to life or physical integrity of others (Article 427, paragraph 1, ZGB). At the end of the three-day period, the patient must be discharged, unless he or she is subject to an enforceable hospitalization order (Article 427, paragraph 2, ZGB). The three-day period begins to run from the point in time when the patient expresses his or her wish to leave the institution and also runs over a weekend and days officially recognized as a public holiday.

E. Medical Procedures

407. According to Article 380 of the ZGB, the treatment of a mental disorder of an incompetent person in a psychiatric clinic is governed exclusively by the provisions on care-related hospitalization. The provisions concerning the representation with regard to medical procedures (Articles 377 et seq., ZGB) do not apply. However, Article 380 of the ZGB applies only to medical procedures for the purpose of treatment of a mental disorder as such. According to the prevailing opinion, if a mentally ill person without power of judgment is suffering from a physical illness, the treatment of that illness falls within the scope of Articles 377 et seq. of the ZGB, even if it is performed in a psychiatric clinic.

408. According to Article 433, paragraph 1, ZGB, a treatment plan must be drawn up. It must be adjusted on a regular basis to take into account ongoing developments (Article 433, paragraph 4, ZGB). The hospitalized patient and, if necessary, a trusted third party must be involved in setting up the treatment plan and briefed on the reasons and purpose of treatment, as well as on possible risks and side effects, alternative treatments, and the possible consequences of forgoing treatment (Article 433, paragraph 2, ZGB).

409. In the case of incompetent patients, an existing advance directive (Articles 370 et seq. ZGB) must be taken into consideration (Article 433, paragraph 3, ZGB). Unlike in the case of a physical illness, in which the advance directive is of binding nature (cf. Article 372, paragraph 2, ZGB), in the context of the treatment of a mental disorder it must 'only' be taken into account. A reasonable treatment cannot be hampered by it (*Botschaft Erwachsenenschutz*, 7068).

410. If the person concerned is competent, his or her consent to a treatment must be obtained. If the person concerned consents to a certain treatment, the treatment is to be performed according to the respective treatment plan.

F. Compulsory Treatment

411. Should the patient refuse to consent to the medical measures in the treatment plan, and should the patient face serious health damage if he or she does not receive medical treatment, or should the life or the physical integrity of a third party be in serious danger, the chief physician may mandate the planned measures. Additionally, the patient must lack power of judgment with regard to the need of treatment, and no other milder measure must be available (Article 434, paragraph 1, ZGB). The patient and a trusted third party must be informed in writing about the order to undergo treatment and must be given instructions about the rights of appeal (Article 434, paragraph 2, ZGB).

412. Unlike a care-related hospitalization, a compulsory treatment interferes not only with the freedom of movement, but also constitutes a severe infringement of the person's physical and mental integrity and thus of personal freedom (Article 10, paragraph 2, BV, and Article 8, no. 1, EHRC). It also clearly violates human dignity (Article 7, BV; see BGE 130 I 16, 18 [2004]; BGE 127 I 6, 10 [2001]). Therefore, the proportionality principle must be observed with particular consideration, and the most sparing measures for the patient must be chosen.

413. Medication, forced feeding, and the enforcement of a daily routine are all possible within the scope of compulsory treatment, but measures and surgical procedures that are controversial or scientifically questionable may not be performed without the patient's consent (*Botschaft Erwachsenenschutz*, 7070).

414. Under certain conditions, measures restraining the freedom of movement, such as fixation or isolation, are also admissible. Article 438 of the ZGB refers insofar to the provisions concerning patients in residential or care institutions (Articles 383 et seq., ZGB). By contrast, sedation must comply with the requirements for compulsory treatment (Article 434, ZGB) because it not only restrains the freedom of movement, but also interferes with physical integrity. The patient has a right to appeal to the court against the restriction of freedom of movement (Article 438, ZGB and Article 439, paragraph 1, no. 5, ZGB).

415. The continuous adjustment of the treatment plan according to ongoing developments (Article 433, paragraph 4, ZGB) is also especially important in the area of compulsory treatment.

G. Emergency Cases

416. According to Article 435 of the ZGB, in cases of emergency medical measures crucial for protecting the patient or third parties may be implemented immediately; however, if they happen to be known, the person's wishes must be taken into consideration (e.g., if there is an advance directive).

H. Legal Protection

417. In cases of hospitalization mandated by a doctor; or when the patient is detained by the institution against his or her will; or when a request of discharge is refused by the institution; or in cases of compulsory treatment of a mental disorder; or in cases of measures restricting the freedom of movement, the patient or a closely related person may appeal in writing to the competent court (Article 439, paragraph 1, ZGB). If the hospitalization is mandated by the adult protection authority, Articles 450 et seq. of the ZGB apply (details regarding deadlines in Article 439, paragraph 2, and Article 450b, paragraph 2, ZGB).

418. The term 'a closely related person' deserves a broad interpretation. According to various decisions of the Swiss Federal Supreme Court, an emotional relationship and the eligibility for safeguarding the interests of the patient are decisive. Parents, the spouse, the registered partner, the life partner, the social worker, a nurse or career, the deputy, or a friend, they all fall within the ambit of the term 'closely related person'.

419. Unless ordered otherwise, the appeal has no suspensive effect (Article 430, paragraph 3, ZGB, Article 450c, ZGB and Article 450e, paragraph 2, ZGB; *Botschaft Erwachsenenschutz*, 7087). A decision must be rendered within five working days of the appeal being filed (Article 450e, paragraph 5, ZGB). As a rule, the court has to hear the person concerned as a panel (Article 450e, paragraph 4, ZGB).

420. In cases involving mental disorders, the decision must be based on the opinion of an expert (Article 450e, paragraph 3, ZGB).

I. Hospitalization and Treatment of Minors

421. According to Article 314b, paragraph 1, of the ZGB, provisions governing the care-related hospitalization of adults (Articles 426 et seq., ZGB) also apply to the hospitalization of a child in a secure institution or a psychiatric clinic.

422. If parents have parental responsibility of the child, the care-related hospitalization amounts to a child protection measure (cf. Article 307, ZGB). As a rule, parental responsibility includes the right to decide on the child's place of residence (Article 301a, paragraph 1, ZGB). A care-related hospitalization without the consent of the parents requires a formal revocation of parental custody according to Article 310, paragraph 1, of the ZGB.

423. Care-related hospitalization of minors suffering from a mental disorder can also be mandated by a doctor authorized by cantonal law (Article 429, ZGB).

424. The treatment of a mental disorder against the will of a minor with power of judgment is, however, precluded. Article 434, paragraph 1, of the ZGB permits compulsory treatment only of incompetent minors. Furthermore, a psychiatric treatment of an incompetent child is only permissible if his or her legal representatives (usually his or her parents) consent to it. With the exception of emergency cases, if the parents reject the medically indicated treatment, the child protection authority must be involved. A competent child may appeal to the court him- or herself (Article 314b, paragraph 2, ZGB).

§3. Stays in Residential or Care Institutions

425. The section of the ZGB on stays in residential or care institutions addresses long-term care of incompetent persons. The section covers provisions about care agreements (Article 382, ZGB), measures restricting the freedom of movement (Articles 383 et seq., ZGB), the protection of privacy (Article 386, ZGB), and the supervision of residential and care institutions (Article 387, ZGB).

I. Care Agreement

426. If an incompetent person is cared for in a residential or care institution for a longer period of time, a written care agreement must be drawn up (Article 382, paragraph 1, ZGB). According to Article 382, paragraph 3, of the ZGB, the representation of the incompetent person in entering, amending, or terminating the care agreement is governed by the provisions on representation in medical matters (Articles 377 et seq., ZGB). With regard to the organization of daily routine, the personal hygiene, the diet, or end-of-life care, the wishes of the person concerned must be taken into account (Article 382, paragraph 2, ZGB). In cases where a person opposes the stay in a residential or care institution, a care-related hospitalization (Articles 426 et seq., ZGB) must be ordered.

II. Measures Restricting Freedom of Movement

427. The residential or care institution may restrict the freedom of movement of the incompetent person only if less stringent measures are clearly insufficient, and the measure serves to prevent serious danger to the life or physical integrity of the person concerned or third parties, or is necessary to remedy serious disruption to community life of the institution (Article 383, ZGB). Such measures restrict the freedom of movement by mechanical means (e.g., electronic surveillance measures, locking of doors, installation of bed rails, fixation or use of security blankets). A measure which can be operated and controlled by the person him- or herself does not fall under this provision. Sedation is not covered by Article 383 of the ZGB. It constitutes an infringement of physical integrity which is why the provisions about legal representation in medical matters (Articles 377 et seq., ZGB) or about compulsory treatment in the context of care-related hospitalization (Article 434, ZGB) apply.

428. Except in emergency cases, the measures and the reasons for them being applied must be explained to the person concerned (Article 383, paragraph 2, ZGB). A measure restricting the freedom of movement must be revoked as soon as possible and in every case reviewed regularly to ascertain whether it is still required (Article 383, paragraph 3, ZGB). Severe infringements of the freedom of movement, such as fixation or isolation, must be limited in time and must be reviewed at least every hour. Measures restricting the freedom of movement must avoid all psychical harm to the person concerned. The residential or care institution must keep a record of all the measures restricting the freedom of movement (Article 384, paragraph 1, ZGB).

429. Furthermore, the institution has an obligation to inform the legal representative of the person concerned about every measure restricting the freedom of movement. The representative has a right to inspect the record at any time (Article 384, paragraph 2, ZGB). However, consent of the representative is not required.

430. The person concerned, his or her representative, or a closely related person may submit a written request to the adult protection authority to intervene (Article 385, paragraph 1, ZGB). The adult protection authority can amend the measure, revoke it, or mandate an adult protection measure.

III. Protection of Personality

431. The residential and care institutions are obliged to protect the personality rights of the incompetent person. Where possible, the residential or care institution must encourage contacts with persons outside the institution (Article 386, paragraph 1, ZGB). If no one outside the institution expresses an interest in the incompetent person, the residential or care institution must notify the adult protection authority (Article 386, paragraph 2, ZGB). The adult protection authority then establishes a deputyship. Moreover, residents of a residential or care institution must be given the opportunity to inform themselves through media. Furthermore, the institution must respect the freedom to choose one's doctor unless there is good reason for not doing so (Article 386, paragraph 3, ZGB), for example in the case of an emergency.

IV. Supervision of Residential and Care Institutions

432. Due to the high vulnerability of the residents, the residential and care institutions are subject to the supervision by the cantons (Article 387, ZGB). The supervisory authority can perform regular and unannounced visits, and it has a right to inspect the records kept by residential or care institutions (Article 384, paragraph 1, ZGB). In addition, the cantons provide for quality standards for residential or care institutions.

§4. The Dying Patient

I. No Special Legal Provisions

433. Dealing with dying patients presents not only a special challenge from a medical and ethical standpoint, but it also raises difficult legal questions. Life is the highest asset of a person and therefore requires special protection, but because Switzerland has no special legal regulations regarding assisted dying, the admissibility and limits of the practice must be derived from the penal code's general provisions.

II. Concepts

434. In conceptual terms, one can speak of assisted dying only if the dying process itself has either begun or looms in the near future. Moreover, assisted dying is performed by third parties (normally the physician) in contrast to cases in which the patient him- or herself – supported by third parties if need be – puts an end to his or her life and is chiefly responsible for those actions. These cases of assisted suicide will be handled in greater detail in Chapter 3, §8 ('Euthanasia').

435. There is a distinction drawn between three forms of assisted dying by means of a third person – i.e., a speeding of the patient's death in terms of an intervening causation: direct assisted dying, indirectly active assisted dying, and passive assisted dying. Directly active assisted dying is the case when the patient's death is deliberately induced (e.g., through administration of a lethal agent) in order to release the patient from his or her suffering. Depending on the motive and circumstances of the deed, directly active assisted suicide comes under the heading of either premeditated murder (Article 111, StGB), voluntary euthanasia (Article 114, StGB), or unlawful homicide (Article 113, StGB). According to the Swiss legal system, it is always illegal, notably also when it occurs at the urgent request of the patient. The admissibility of directly active assisted dying could only be achieved through a change in the law; various attempts have been undertaken in this regard but the prohibition of directly active assisted dying is largely adhered to.

436. Indirectly active assisted dying is the case when the intention is to relieve the patient's suffering through the use of medication whose side effects can shorten the patient's life. The side effects of these medications are apparently far rarer than hitherto assumed (see SAMW-*Richtlinien zur Betreuung von Patientinnen und Patienten am Lebensende* [2004, updated 2012], no. 3.1) and are accepted for the sake of achieving the desired main objective – the relief of suffering and the increase in a patient's quality of life. There are no express legal provisions for this form of assisted dying. It could actually be subsumed under the heading of homicide with indirect intent. But because relieving a patient's suffering is the physician's recognized professional duty (see SAMW-*Richtlinien zur Betreuung von Patientinnen und Patienten am Lebensende* [2004, updated 2012], no. 3.1), indirectly active assisted dying is judged as permissible as long as administration of the medications remains within the requisite parameters. Nevertheless, there occasionally emerge delicate problems of demarcation between directly and indirectly active assisted dying, since its ascription to one category or the other depends solely on the doctor's intent. This intent can be inferred, for example, by means of the applied agent's dosage (SAMW-*Richtlinien zur Betreuung von Patientinnen und Patienten am Lebensende* [2004, updated 2012], no. 3.1).

437. In the final analysis, passive assisted dying is the case if life-sustaining measures are eschewed or broken off – e.g., if artificial respiration is discontinued. One speaks of passive assisted dying in such cases since the physician allows the death to run its natural course without attempting (or without continuing) to obstruct it through extraordinary medical measures. An explicit provision for this form of assisted dying is also lacking in the law; however, negligent homicide is indeed covered. Because in the contractual relationship to his or her patient the doctor is, as a rule, criminally liable – i.e., the physician is responsible for the legally protected right of the patient to 'life and health' – he or she can also principally fulfil the conditions pursuant to cases of homicide (according to Article 111 of the StGB) through omission of the requisite life-sustaining measures insofar as the physician would indeed have been in a position to thereby save the patient's life. But passive assisted dying is fundamentally permissible if the available medical measures are unable to substantially prolong the patient's life. However, if the patient's death can be postponed for a longer period through the use of extraordinary medical measures (e.g., through mechanical respiration), then passive dying assistance is permissible contingent on the patient's wishes or, if this is lacking, on the patient's presumed wishes.

III. The Patient's Wishes as a Criterion of Permissible Action

438. The patient's desires are the primary criterion for the type of medical measures to be taken by the doctor or nurse with regard to terminally ill or dying patients and hence also the various forms of permissible assisted dying. Respect for the patient's right to self-determination also encompasses a respect for his or her rejection of vitally needed medical treatment. Mentally competent patients thus decide for themselves whether and for how long they wish to have life-sustaining and perhaps very invasive treatment. The prerequisite for a valid rejection of vital medical measures is thorough briefing of the patient regarding his or her situation and prognosis.

IV. Incompetent Patients

439. A more problematic situation is that of a patient who is mentally incompetent due to age or illness and therefore can no longer make a decision as to whether he or she desires further life-sustaining measures.

440. The rules concerning legal representation with regard to medical procedures described above (cf. Chapter 1, §2. Informed Consent) apply likewise in case of terminally ill patients. An advance directive must be consulted and is legally binding so that the doctor must comply with it, unless it violates statutory regulations or there is reasonable doubt that it is based on the patient's free will or still corresponds to his or her presumed will (Article 372, paragraph 2, ZGB). An advance directive violates statutory provisions if, for instance, the advance directive asks for direct active assisted dying (cf. Article 111, StGB, Article 114, StGB or Article 113, StGB). A decision not to comply with the advance directive has to be explained in the medical records of the patient (Article 372, paragraph 2, ZGB).

441. In an advance directive, a person can also authorize another person to make upcoming decisions regarding life-sustaining measures, after having been duly provided with the necessary information by the attending physician, and give the person instructions (Article 370, paragraph 2 and 3, ZGB).

442. If the patient has not given any instructions on life-sustaining measures, or the advance directive is for whatever reason invalid, the attending doctor must plan the required treatment in consultation with the legal representative of the patient (Article 377, paragraph 1, Article 378 ZGB, cf. also Article 6 of the Biomedicine Convention). The legal representative of the patient must decide on the basis of the patient's presumed will and interests. Guiding principles for the presumed will are derived from earlier statements to relatives, caregivers, or the primary care physician. In the case of any ambiguity, the patient's general value system can be enlisted to determine his or her presumed will. Unlike the patient's presumed will, the interests are determined by objective medical criteria, including the estimated quality of life of the patient.

443. Swiss Civil Law does not specify if the patient's presumed will or his or her interests take priority in case of a contradiction between the two. However, if the decision to be taken contradicts the patient's objective interests, there must be convincing reasons for doing so; meaning that the patient's presumed will is ascertained. Moreover, it is highly questionable whether it is always in the objective interests of the patient to postpone the time of death as long as possible, particularly in cases where medical treatment is available, but there is no reasonable hope of a cure or benefit (so-called futile medical treatment).

444. According to Article 381, paragraph 1, of the ZGB, the adult protection authority (*Erwachsenenschutzbehörde*) establishes a representative deputyship (*Vertretungsbeistandschaft*), if there is no representative available or the representative does not wish to exercise the right to act. If it is unclear who has a right to act as a legal representative, or the persons with a right to act as legal representatives are unable to agree, the adult protection authority appoints a representative or, again, establishes a representative deputyship (Article 381, paragraph 2, ZGB). The adult protection authority acts thereby at the request of the doctor, a person closely associated with the patient, or ex officio (Article 381, paragraph 3, ZGB). The doctor or another person closely associated with the patient can advise the adult protection authority, if he or she is of the opinion that a certain measurement is not compatible with the patient's presumed will and interests (Article 381, paragraph 2, no. 3, ZGB).

V. Palliative Care

445. With respect to the treatment of terminally ill and dying patients, in the last several years so-called palliative care has increasingly been the focus of attention, not least owing to the fact that no social consensus could be reached with regard to assisted dying. The need for action in caring for the terminally ill and dying became manifest after the general public became aware of the suicides of terminally ill patients and the assisted suicide offered by certain entities dedicated to such and organized under private law. Demands for the development and funding of palliative care were informed not only by medical concerns but by legal and political ones as well. The goal was both an increase in the quality of life of terminally ill patients and, in particular, a reduction in the number of suicides within this group.

446. 'Palliative care' means the all-encompassing medical, nursing, social, psychological, and emotional care of the terminally ill or those patients suffering from a chronic and progressive affliction. It aims to diminish suffering and increase the patient's quality of life. In particular, palliative care is found in the spheres of neonatology, intensive-care medicine, geriatrics, and psychiatry (SAWM-Richtlinien Palliative Care [2006, updated 2012], 6). Palliative care may also encompass indirectly active assisted dying, i.e., the use of medication with the intention to relieve the patient's suffering, despite it shortening the patient's life as a side effect.

447. Individual cantonal laws make explicit mention of the right to palliative medicine – i.e., the right to decent caregiving and attendance while dying. However, the kind of palliative care on offer varies from canton to canton and from region to region. In recent years, however, palliative care has been promoted and developed. With enactment of the *Bundesgesetz über die universitären Medizinalberufe* (MedBG, Federal Law on University Medical Professions), which went into effect on 1 September 2007, training in palliative care was integrated into educational and advanced training goals (Article 6, paragraph 1a, MedBG). Guidelines and a National Strategy 'Palliative Care' 2010–2012 and 2013–2015, under the direction of the Federal Health Office (*Bundesamt für Gesundheit, BAG*), show the commitment of making palliative care more accessible for the seriously and terminally ill patients. The 'National Guidelines Palliative Care', as cornerstone of the National Strategy, define palliative care, describe the basic values, targeted group, location of treatment and palliative care providers.

Chapter 3. Specific Activities

§1. Abortion

I. Overview of Legal Foundations

448. The provisions governing abortion are to be found in the StGB. Articles 118, 119, and 120 of the StGB regulate the criminal liability of abortion, the conditions that must be fulfilled for it to be legal, as well as the criminal consequences of a breach of medical duty. The aforementioned articles protect unborn human life during pregnancy as well as the pregnant woman's health and right to self-determination. According to prevailing opinion, criminal protection of the unborn begins after the fertilized egg has implanted itself in the womb (nidation). As soon as the birthing process begins (according to prevailing opinion, this starts with the onset of labour pains), the abortion laws are no longer in play but rather those addressing homicide and criminal assault (Articles 111 et seq., StGB).

449. Article 118 of the StGB categorically makes abortion a punishable offence. The termination of a pregnancy becomes punishable if the stated conditions in Article 119 of the StGB for legality are not fulfilled or if a pregnancy is terminated without the consent of the pregnant woman.

450. Article 119 of the StGB deals with the conditions for legal abortion. Paragraph 1 of the provision contains the 'indication rule', whereby the abortion is exempt from punishment should a certain medical or socio-medical condition be met. Paragraph 2 contains the 'time-limit rule', whereby the termination of a pregnancy may be carried out with impunity if the abortion occurs within twelve weeks after start of the woman's last period. From a legal theoretical standpoint, both of these sub-provisions supply grounds of justification for an abortion so that it will not come under the category of 'illicit'.

451. And, last, Article 120 of the StGB punishes individual breaches of duty by physicians in connection with abortions on the basis of the twelve-week rule (Article 119, paragraph 2, StGB). This provision describes a genuine special offence, as only a doctor can commit this crime.

II. Punishable Abortions, Article 118 of the StGB

452. This article dictates the conditions under which the premeditated abortion is punishable. The pregnant woman may terminate her pregnancy or have it terminated with impunity within a period of twelve weeks after the start of her last menstruation. After expiration of this period, she is punishable if the condition discussed in Article 119, paragraph 1, of the StGB is not met. The penalty is a prison term of up to three years or a fine.

453. Third parties make themselves liable to persecution if they abort a pregnancy without the consent of the woman concerned (penalty: a prison sentence of between one and ten years) or if they abort the pregnancy with her consent but without one of the conditions for legality in Article 119 of the StGB being met (penalty: a prison term of up to three years or a fine). In addition, third parties who aid and abet the abortion are also punishable.

III. Legal Abortion, Article 119 of the StGB

A. *Time-Limit Rule in Article 119, Paragraph 2, of the StGB*

454. According to Article 119, paragraph 2, of the StGB, an abortion is not subject to punishment if it meets the following conditions: it must be undertaken within twelve weeks of the beginning of the woman's last menstruation; the pregnant woman must request the abortion in writing and confirm that an emergency situation exists; the abortion must be performed by a licensed doctor; and the doctor must have a personal counselling interview with the pregnant woman before the abortion. The written request and the counselling interview are mere regulatory actions whose non-fulfilment constitutes a misdemeanour (Article 120, paragraph 1, StGB).

455. From an international perspective, the time frame within which abortions are permitted is rather small, allowing the pregnant woman only a relatively short period to consider her options. Should the twelve-week period be exceeded, a legal abortion is only possible if a certain medical or socio-medical condition has been met, as detailed in Article 119, paragraph 1, of the StGB. The pregnant woman must request the abortion in writing, with the initiative thus taken by the woman. According to the law, the pregnant woman must claim that an emergency situation exists, but this need not be further explained – the 'emergency situation' need not be an objective fact confirmed by an expert. It is sufficient for the pregnant woman to inform her doctor that she finds herself in an emergency situation. There will be no official inquiry into whether her assertion accords with the facts of the case. Moreover, the absence of this prerequisite does not make the abortion illegal. Every licensed physician can perform the abortion; the physician need not be a gynaecologist or surgeon. The minimum content in the personal counselling session as required by Article 119, paragraph 1, of the StGB, is detailed in Article 120, paragraph 1b, which requires a thorough counselling interview that imparts information regarding the health risks entailed in the procedure. Moreover, the pregnant woman must be given a handbook against receipt that catalogues free information centres and contains a list of associations and centres that offer moral and material assistance as well as information regarding the alternative of putting her unborn child up for adoption. The law provides for no waiting period between the counselling session and the abortion itself, which can be performed immediately following the interview.

B. Indication Provision in Article 119, Paragraph 1, of the StGB

456. Article 119, paragraph 1, of the StGB deals with the conditions for an abortion to be legal even if performed after expiration of the twelve-week period as detailed in Article 119, paragraph 2. According to this clause, an abortion can be undertaken with impunity if there is a medical necessity – e.g., the pregnant woman is threatened with serious physical harm (medical indication) or with the infliction of grave mental distress (socio-medical indication) that can be averted through the abortion. The more advanced the pregnancy, the greater must be the danger. An abortion on the basis of an indication remains possible up until the onset of birthing pangs. Because the law considers it self-evident, there is no specific mention that the pregnant woman must always give her consent – the only exception being a mentally incompetent woman, in which case the provisions regarding presumed acquiescence with regard to exculpatory contingencies are to be applied.

457. As the law does not specify who may undertake an abortion, it is unclear as to whether laypersons or, for example, midwives can perform an abortion, provided that a doctor deems it necessary. As in Article 119, paragraph 2, of the StGB, prevailing opinion assumes that only a licensed doctor is eligible to do so.

458. A physician must judge whether a medical or socio-medical indication is present. The doctor who ascertains the indication may undertake the abortion him- or herself. The law does not require that a second opinion be obtained. Prevailing opinion would have it that the embryopathic indication can be included in the category of a socio-medical indication – i.e., an abortion on the basis of the unborn's physical or mental disorders, which would lead, postnatally, to a serious burden being placed on the mother. A criminological indication is also permissible – i.e., aborting a pregnancy that has been engendered through criminal activity (e.g., rape).

C. Abortion in the Case of Minors or the Mentally Incompetent

459. A pregnant and mentally competent minor may and must request an abortion herself, as this is a strictly personal right. She may also conclude a corresponding contract for treatment on her own, since the costs of treatment are reimbursed by medical insurance.

460. In the case of mental incompetence, the legal representative must give his or her consent (Article 119, paragraph 3, StGB). This is determined by the system of law for abortion on the basis of the time-limit provision as well as the provisions on indications. While it is uncontested that the incompetent pregnant woman's legal representative may consent to an abortion along lines of a medical or socio-medical indication, there is no consensus among legal scholars as to whether the representative may request an abortion on the basis of the time-limit provision. Prevailing opinion says yes, but some hold the opposite view, as an abortion on the basis of the time-limit provision is not a medically indicated measure but rather a concession to the pregnant woman's right of self-determination.

D. Duty to Inform

461. Article 119, paragraph 5, of the StGB specifies that any doctor undertaking an abortion has a duty to notify the authorities. While fully preserving doctor-patient confidentiality and the anonymity of the concerned woman, every abortion must be reported. The purpose of this notification is to enable statistics to be kept on the number of abortions.

§2. STERILIZATION

462. As of 1 July 2005, there has been a special legal basis for sterilization for purposes of contraception in Switzerland: the *Sterilisationsgesetz* (Sterilisation Law) governing the requirements and procedures of sterilization. The law defines sterilization as a medical procedure that permanently eliminates a person's procreative capability (Article 2, paragraph 1, *Sterilisationsgesetz*). But the law's scope extends to sterilizations for birth control purposes only and expressly not for therapeutic procedures whose unavoidable side effect is the removal of one's ability to procreate (Article 2, paragraph 2, *Sterilisationsgesetz*). As always, these are to be judged according to the general rules pertaining to therapeutic procedures.

463. First of all, the law fundamentally prohibits the sterilization of persons under age 18 (exceptions can be found in Article 7, *Sterilisationsgesetz*) and of those persons over 18 years of age who are mentally incompetent on a temporary basis (Articles 3 et seq., *Sterilisationsgesetz*). The sterilization of incompetent persons over the age of 18 is permitted so long as these individuals are comprehensively informed as to the procedure beforehand and they have freely given their consent in writing. But the individual's competence must not be simply presumed but positively substantiated in the patient's medical records (Article 5, *Sterilisationsgesetz*).

464. According to Article 6 of the Sterilisation Law, those competent persons who are legally incapacitated may be sterilized as long as all of the following prerequisites are fulfilled: The person must be over 18 years of age, must be thoroughly informed as to the procedure, must consent to the procedure of his or her own free will and in writing, and his or her legal representative must likewise grant consent. Here, too, the person's competence must be affirmed and substantiated in the patient's medical records. Additionally, before the sterilization, consent of the custodial supervising authority must be obtained.

465. The sterilization of persons over 16 years of age who are mentally incompetent on a permanent basis is permissible in exceptional cases and if certain narrow conditions are met in full (Article 7, *Sterilisationsgesetz*). First, sterilization is only possible if the concerned person is unlikely to ever recover his or her mental competence. It also must be affirmed that the procedure is in the overall interest of the concerned person. In this regard, it is only the well-being of the concerned person that plays a role, not the interests of third parties. Moreover, there must be reason to expect that a child will be conceived and carried to term, and that this cannot be prevented by other appropriate methods of birth control or the voluntary sterilization of the mentally competent partner. According to the principle of subsidiarity, sterilization of an incompetent person is a last resort in terms of birth control. But even in this case sterilization is only then permissible if, after the birth, separation from the child is unavoidable because parental responsibility could not be assumed or because the pregnancy of the concerned woman would substantially threaten her health. In any event, the method of operation to be chosen is that with the best prospects of re-fertilization. And finally, the custodial supervising authority must give its consent to the sterilization. Although the draft law contained a veto right for incompetent persons, this was dropped; it was an attempt to attest to the absolutely binding nature of the 'natural desire' of the incompetent person.

466. The concerned person, someone close to concerned person, his or her guardian, or the guardianship authority can call upon the custodial supervising authority to verify whether the conditions for a sterilization have been met. Before any decision, the custodial supervising authority is required by federal law to hear out – separately – the person concerned as well as those persons closest to that person, to have an expert report issued on the social and personal relationships of the person concerned, and to have the incompetence and the duration of this state clarified in an expert medical report (Article 8, *Sterilisationsgesetz*).

467. The decision of the custodial supervising authority can be contested in court by the person concerned, by a person close to that person, or by his or her guardian (Article 9, *Sterilisationsgesetz*). The notion of 'a person close to that person' is not to be ascertained by means of rigid precepts; rather, what is crucial here is the strength of the bond (*Bericht Zwangssterilisationen*, 6333).

468. To conclude, Article 10 of the Sterilisation Law imposes a duty to provide anonymous data to the authorities, thus allowing for the compilation of statistics with regard to the sterilization of those persons who are legally incapacitated or are in a permanent state of incompetence. First of all, the sterilization of such persons is to afterwards be reported to an office determined by cantonal law. Additionally, the law provides for a retroactive reporting duty for the effectuation of therapeutic procedures on incompetent persons whose unavoidable side effect is elimination of the ability to procreate. The addressee in this case is the custodial supervising authority. This reporting duty serves a pre-emptive purpose and is designed to prevent unregulated sterilizations performed on mentally handicapped persons for the purpose of birth control but that are carried out under the pretence of a medical indication so as to bypass the conditions of Article 7 of the Sterilisation Law (*Bericht Zwangssterilisation*, 6336).

§3. In Vitro Fertilization

I. Constitutional Principles

469. Article 119 of the Swiss Federal Constitution contains provisions on reproductive health. Paragraph 1, Article 119, of the Swiss Federal Constitution specifies that people must be protected from the abuses of reproductive medicine. Paragraph 2, Article 119, of the Swiss Federal Constitution grants the federal government wide-ranging powers to issue provisions for dealing with human gametes and germ cells. In particular, protection of human dignity, personality, and the family is to be guaranteed. At the same time, it is emphasized that reproductive health procedures are meant to promote families (*Botschaft Fortpflanzungsmedizingesetz*, 246). And finally, paragraph 2a–g, Article 119, of the Swiss Federal Constitution contains detailed substantive provisions governing reproductive health. First of all, any such medically supported reproductive procedures can only be applied as a subsidiary measure if either infertility or the danger of transmission of a serious illness exists and if these conditions cannot be otherwise remedied. But these procedures are inadmissible for research purposes only or if they are carried out to produce certain characteristics in the child. In contrast to certain of its European neighbours, Switzerland allows human ova to be developed into embryos outside the woman's body, but stipulates that their number must not exceed those that are required for medically assisted reproduction. Before the popular vote on 14 June 2015 Article 119, paragraph 2, letter c, BV allowed only to develop as many egg cells into embryos as could be immediately implanted. This relaxation of the strict limitation of the number of embryos that may be produced allows the realization of preimplantation diagnostics in terms of constitutional law. Through the limitation of the number of embryos that may be developed, the problem of surplus embryos is avoided. On the other hand, it is permissible to take more ova than needed and to freeze them at the pronucleus stage – i.e., before cell union (*Botschaft Fortpflanzungsmedizingesetz*, 215). Even if the embryo's legal status is not thereby completely clarified, the constitution does grant the embryo protection of its dignity, health, and life for its own sake (if only partial protection, naturally, in these latter two cases). Yet, according to prevailing opinion, the embryo has no right to life. The constitution is also restrictive in terms of embryo donors and surrogate mothers. Both procedures are prohibited in Switzerland since, according to Swiss legal views, they contradict the principle of respect for human dignity and a child's well-being. Furthermore, the constitution contains a ban on the commercialization of human germ cells and embryo products and assures all persons access to data regarding their parentage. Therefore, the sperm donor's anonymity is not legally guaranteed.

II. Federal Law on Medically Supported Reproduction

470. The *Bundesgesetz über die medizinisch unterstützte Fortpflanzung* (FMedG), or Medical Reproduction Law, in force since 1 January 2001, governs the admissibility requirements of medically supported human reproduction procedures (Article 1, paragraph 1, FMedG). According to the legal definition as elaborated in Article 2 a of the Medical Reproduction Law, 'medically supported human reproduction' refers to methods of inducing a pregnancy without sexual intercourse, in particular through artificial insemination, in vitro fertilization together with an embryo transfer, as well as a gamete transfer. Not coming under the law's application is the purely hormonal therapy used to treat infertility.

471. Reproductive procedures may only be employed, first of all, when the child's welfare is guaranteed (Article 3, paragraph 1, FMedG). Second, reproduction procedures are reserved for couples for whom a legal parent-child relationship can be justified. Single mothers or same-sex partners therefore have no access to medically supported reproduction procedures. This remains the case even if the same-sex partners have entered into a registered partnership similar to marriage, as contained in Article 28 of the Partnership Law. The reason for this is that the law upholds the fundamental condition of human existence, namely that every child has a mother and father who have a specific impact on the development of a child (*Botschaft Fortpflanzungsmedizingesetz*, 250). Further, on the basis of their age and their personal relationship, the couple desiring to be parents must be able to bring up and care for the child until it has reached maturity. The Federal Council's documentation justifies this precondition insofar as that, in the case of medically supported reproduction as opposed to natural procreation, there are third parties involved whose actions must be justified from the standpoint of the child's welfare (*Botschaft Fortpflanzungsmedizingesetz*, 249). In Switzerland, fertilization using the sperm cells of third parties – so-called heterologous insemination – is reserved for married couples (Article 3, paragraph 3, FMedG). In order to prevent children from being conceived after the death of their parents and to avoid children even being born of unborn 'parents', Article 3, paragraph 4, of the Medical Reproduction Law forbids the use of gametes or impregnated ova after the death of the person to whom they belong. At most, so as to protect the life of the embryo, an embryo transfer shortly after the father's death is deemed permissible (*Botschaft Fortpflanzungsmedizingesetz*, 253).

472. Along with the constitutional prohibition on embryo donation and surrogate motherhood, the Reproductive Health Law also forbids egg donation – which is occasionally viewed as discriminatory against women (Article 4, FMedG). The law justifies this prohibition with the argument that any split between genetic and biological motherhood should be prevented, as there is no analogy to be found in nature for such a situation. By contrast, heterological insemination has a natural parallel, for it is not uncommon that the husband and legal father of a child is not the genetic father (*Botschaft Fortpflanzungsmedizingesetz*, 245 et seq.).

473. The selection of gametes with respect to the child's sex or characteristics may only take place to prevent the transmission of a serious and incurable affliction. Eugenically motivated selections are therefore forbidden in Switzerland (Article 119, paragraph 2 c, BV). Moreover, because of the danger of its misuse, Preimplantation Genetic Diagnosis (PGD) has so far been prohibited in Switzerland (Article 5, paragraph 2, FMedG), however, this changed recently (cf. Chapter 3, §4.II.).

474. The law permits the selection of donated sperm cells according to blood type and the donor's physical similarities to the child's prospective future father (Article 5, paragraph 2, and Article 22, paragraph 4, FMedG). This is a concession to the parents' power to make such choices and helps promote the fiction of natural conception.

475. The law contains detailed provisions on the counselling and information given to the prospective parents, who must provide their consent in writing and also observe a waiting period (Article 6 and Article 7, paragraph 1, FMedG). The consent can be revoked in writing at any time, at which point the gametes are to be immediately destroyed. In each case, consent must be renewed after three cycles of treatment, and it must also be given anew if impregnated ova are intended to be reactivated after cryopreservation (Article 7, paragraph 1 and 2, FMedG). If there is the risk of a multiple pregnancy, the procedure may only be carried out if the couple agrees to a multiple birth (Article 7, paragraph 3, FMedG). In principle, ova can be conserved for a maximum of five years and then must be destroyed; but a longer period of conservation can be agreed upon with persons who undergo treatment by a physician or who have an occupation that can lead to infertility or damage to the genotype (Article 15, FMedG). Impregnated ova can be conserved for five years at most and only under the condition that they be used at a later date to induce a pregnancy (Article 16, paragraph 1b, FMedG). In this case, too, consent can be revoked at any time by either of the prospective parents, at which point the impregnated ova must be immediately destroyed.

476. The Reproductive Health Law permits a maximum of three embryos to be developed outside a woman's body, but only to the extent necessary to induce a pregnancy (Article 17, paragraph 1, FMedG). The preservation of these embryos was forbidden (Article 17, paragraph 3, FMedG). This changed with the vote in June 2016 (cf. Chapter 3, §4.II.). In the future, it will be possible to store embryos so that they can be transferred to the womb at a later date if required.

477. In order to ensure the necessary monitoring, the law holds suppliers responsible for authorizing and reporting any reproductive health procedures, and it defines the conditions for authorization (Articles 8 et seq., FMedG). An authorization agency supervises the physicians active in this sphere as well.

478. A special section of the law is devoted to sperm donors (Articles 18 et seq., FMedG). The law regulates donor selection, which must be made from a medical standpoint only. In addition, it stipulates the free donation of sperm and the restricted use of donated sperm cells, which, among other things, is intended to prevent subsequent incestuous relationships. In Switzerland, a sperm donor's anonymity is not guaranteed. In this respect, the law strikes the balance in favour of the right to know its own origin (cf. Article 119, paragraph, 2 g, BV). Therefore, the donor must be informed in writing that upon completion of the child's 18th year, the child can demand information regarding his or her parentage and hence particulars as to the donor (Article 18, paragraph 2, and Article 27, FMedG). The child may even demand information earlier if he or she has an interest meriting protection, such as health concerns. However, the child may not bring an action against the sperm donor so as to ascertain his paternity or contest his legal parent-child relationship with the child's mother's husband (Article 23, FMedG). The mother's data and that of the sperm donor must be documented and, after the child's (presumed) birth, transmitted to the Swiss Federal Office for Births, Marriages and Deaths (Article 24 and Article 25, FMedG). The prospective future parents have no right to know any particulars, and the sperm donor himself is not allowed access to information regarding any potential children.

479. Finally, the law provides for sanctions on the prohibited abuse of reproductive health procedures (Articles 29 et seq., FMedG).

§4. Prenatal Diagnosis (Genetics in General)

I. Gene Technology and Reproduction: Constitutional Principles

480. Article 119 of the Swiss Federal Constitution concerns itself with the fundamental regulation of gene technology in the human sphere. As the norm to be achieved, Article 119, paragraph 1, of the Swiss Federal Constitution states that individuals should be protected from any misuses of gene technology, and the legislators decided on a certain concept of misuse: Gene technology in the human sphere is fundamentally allowed, while misuses should be averted. Paragraph 2 provides for comprehensive federal authority and a binding mandate for federal legislators to enact regulations for dealing with human gametes and germ cells. This authority encompasses all those actions involving human gametes and germ cells that bear on human dignity, personality, or the family, irrespective of whether these actions are carried out within the scope of medical treatments or for research purposes.

481. The constitution forbids all manner of cloning and all procedures involving manipulation of the gametes of human germ cells and embryos. It is in this sense that the constitution recognizes a 'fundamental right to gametes that are not artificially altered'. Also excluded in this regard is germline therapy. Non-human gametes and germ cells may not be introduced into or combined with human germ cells. Thus, human germ cells, as the fundament of human life, must be protected from any attempt to combine them with animal gametes.

II. Prenatal Screenings and Preimplantation Genetic Diagnoses

482. The mere study of embryonic cells, for example, within the framework of a prenatal screening or PGD, is not regarded as a procedure impacting gametes as elaborated in Article 119, paragraph 2a, of the Swiss Federal Constitution. Thus, prenatal screenings and preimplantation genetic diagnoses are in principle permissible because they are in line with the constitution. At the same time, there are restrictions in place at the statutory law level, particularly the *Bundesgesetz über genetische Untersuchungen beim Menschen* (GUMG), or Federal Law on Genetic Tests on Humans.

483. The GUMG employs the phrase 'prenatal test' as the umbrella term for prenatal genetic examinations and prenatal risk assessments. Prenatal tests for risks are laboratory tests that provide information on possible genetic abnormalities. They also include examinations of the embryo or foetus using imaging processes (Article 3g, GUMG). The prenatal test for risks is not a genetic test, but as its purpose is to discover any genetic abnormalities in the unborn child, it can function as a preliminary stage to such a test (see *Botschaft* GUMG, 7419). In contrast to the prenatal test for risks, for example ultrasound, prenatal genetic tests may not be routinely offered (see *Botschaft* GUMG, 7410). Important in connection with prenatal tests is also the prohibition on mass screenings, for which no early treatment or prevention measures are possible (Article 12, GUMG).

484. According to Article 11 of the GUMG, prenatal tests may not be carried out to ascertain characteristics of the embryo or foetus that do not directly compromise its health, or so as to determine its sex for reasons other than diagnosing a medical condition. Before and after the prenatal genetic and family-planning tests (which, according to the law, are genetic tests for discovering any genetic risks for future offspring; Article 3h, GUMG), non-directive expert advice must be proffered in a genetic briefing and documented (Article 14, GUMG). The counselling session must be limited to individual and familial interests and not address general social interests. In this way, the danger of eugenic tendencies can be averted (see *Botschaft* GUMG, 7415). The scope of the genetic briefing is substantially greater than that entailed by the usual duty to explain an upcoming medical procedure (*Botschaft* GUMG, 7414). The briefing is designed to detail any possible mental and social repercussions of the test result on the individual concerned and his or her family. The Federal Council regards the briefing as enabling the person concerned to make an independent decision for or against the genetic test (see *Botschaft* GUMG, 7415). The law contains binding provisions with regard to the frame of reference and the most important elements of the conversation. If an undesirable finding is likely to be non-treatable by therapeutic or prophylactic means, then the pregnant woman must be duly informed prior to the test. The pregnant woman must be conscious of the fact that in such a case an abortion is the only possible way of averting the birth of a disabled or sick child and that consequently this test does not serve to promote the health of the unborn child (see *Botschaft* GUMG, 7418). If possible, the woman's partner should be included in the briefings. It is also stipulated that there be a waiting period between the briefing and the test itself, which should be individually determined.

485. Both before and after the prenatal genetic test ('after' meaning after the results are in), the pregnant woman must be explicitly informed as to her right of self-determination. After the briefing, she decides whether or not she would like to undertake a prenatal test, whether she would like to be informed as to the test result, and what she wishes to do based on it. This means that her right to not knowing is also explicitly protected (Article 6, GUMG), as the pregnant woman can insist on not being informed of the test result. But the law provides for an exception: the pregnant woman must be promptly informed of the research result if there exists for herself or the embryo or the foetus a directly threatening physical risk that could be averted (Article 18, paragraph 2, GUMG). Consent to a prenatal genetic test and the family-planning tests must be given in writing.

486. If the findings point to a serious and incurable disorder, the woman must be informed of the alternatives to abortion and be made aware of other counselling options.

487. Furthermore, in all prenatal briefings on the risks entailed, the woman must be informed beforehand as to the purpose and significance of the test, and she must also be made aware of the possibility of an unexpected test result, possible follow-up tests, and the independent cantonal information and counselling centres (Article 16, GUMG).

488. While the fundamental permissibility of prenatal screenings is not questioned, in terms of the Reproductive Health Law the legislators decided to explicitly prohibit PGD: Article 5, paragraph 3, of the Reproductive Health Law forbids the removal of one or several cells from an embryo in vitro and their analysis. PGD is a procedure to examine the genetic material of embryos before being implanted into the uterus for purposes of artificial fertilization (in vitro fertilization, IVF), which requires the extraction of embryonic cells and aims at ensuring that the prospective child will not suffer from a serious hereditary condition. The prohibition is based on the fact that the long-term effects of a PGD for the embryo are unknown and there is the additional danger of misdiagnoses. Moreover, the legislators expressed the fear that embryos could be increasingly selected according to a wide variety of criteria, thereby blurring the lines between permissible prevention and unwanted selection in the future. Apart from that, in the case of PGD – in contrast to prenatal screening – the legislators feel that there would be a risk of selections being made if findings are negative (see *Botschaft Fortpflanzungsmedizingesetz*, 257).

489. In 2004, with the initiative 'admission of preimplantation genetic diagnosis' the parliament tasked the Swiss Federal Council 'to put forward a regulation that enables PGD and stipulates the conditions under which it may take place'. The Federal Council completed the preliminary work on the new regulation and passed the draft legislation to the Federal Assembly. The draft legislation permitted PGD but only under strict requirements. It provided that PGD could only be applied in order to prevent a serious incurable hereditary condition carried by the parents. The outbreak of that serious hereditary illness had to occur before the person concerned turned 50. Moreover, the application of PGD for the purposes other than the prevention of a serious hereditary condition constituted a punishable offence. Parliamentary deliberation in 2014 on the Federal Council's draft bill resulted in a much more liberal legislation. The constitutional amendment necessary because of the former restriction of the number of embryos allowed to be developed in vitro to three was adopted by the majority of the people and the cantons in a mandatory popular vote on 14 June 2015. The amendments will come into force as soon as the relevant ordinances are amended as well.

490. Unlike the initial Federal Council's draft, the amended Reproductive Health Law opens PGD to all couples undergoing medically assisted reproduction procedures for the purpose of screening for chromosomal aberrations that could impair the development of the embryo. For the purposes of functional PGD, the amended Reproductive Health Law allows to develop up to twelve embryos in vitro.

III. Genetic Tests on Humans in the Medical Sphere

491. Article 119, paragraphs 2 et seq., of the Swiss Federal Constitution states that a person's gametes can only be analysed, recorded, or disclosed with his or her permission. The law can provide for exceptions. This constitutes explicit constitutional protection of the fundamental right to the protection of privacy or informational self-determination (see *Botschaft* GUMG, 7376). Additionally, the federal government is granted wide-ranging powers to enact provisions governing human gametes, whereby it is specifically responsible for protecting human dignity, personality rights, and the family (Article 119, paragraph 2, BV).

492. With enactment of the GUMG, which became effective 1 April 2007, the federal government made use of its legislative powers in the area of gene technology in the human sphere. The law states the conditions under which genetic tests on humans may be undertaken in the medical, work, and insurance spheres and also addresses third-party liability. Furthermore, it regulates the creation of DNA profiles for clarifying ancestry or identifying persons. The concept of testing, on the one hand, must be understood in a broad sense, embracing not only the actual analysis of the biological sample but also the counselling session, obtaining the consent, taking the sample, communicating the findings, and preserving or using the sample (see *Botschaft* GUMG, 7387). On the other hand, in the legal definition of Article 3a of the GUMG, the law limits the concept of genetic testing to analyses whose purpose is to obtain information on the hereditary characteristics – or those acquired in the embryonal phase – of a person's gametes. Therefore, not falling within this category is the test for retroactively emergent pathological changes to the gametes, as can, for example, be manifested within the framework of cancer (*Botschaft* GUMG, 7287). Also not falling within the scope of the law (Article 1, paragraph 3, GUMG; see *Botschaft* GUMG, 7388) are genetic studies on humans that take place within the framework of research projects, including genetic population studies. These are regulated in the HFG. The GUMG aims to protect human dignity and personality rights, defend against misuses in the area of genetic tests, and prevent the deployment of any genetic data thus acquired. Furthermore, the quality of the tests and the interpretation of the findings must be assured (Article 2, GUMG).

493. For genetic tests, the GUMG adheres to the primary principle that discrimination based on genotype is impermissible (Article 4, GUMG). This principle has not only the state but also the private sector in view (see *Botschaft* GUMG, 7396). Only physicians are allowed to initiate genetic analyses; at the same time, a genetic briefing must be ensured (Article 13, GUMG). This provision is justified by reason of the great impact that the findings of any genetic test can have on the life of the concerned individual (see *Botschaft* GUMG, 7403). Therefore, the free sale of genetic in vitro diagnostics to unauthorized persons is likewise forbidden (Article 9, GUMG).

494. Genetic analyses may only be undertaken for medical purposes and must ensure the person's right of self-determination (Article 10, paragraph 1, GUMG). This right can only be exercised after a sufficient briefing and includes, first, the right to decide whether any genetic analysis should be undertaken at all, and, second, the right to decide whether one wants to be informed of the test's findings. Thus, along with the right to informational self-determination, the right to ignorance is also explicitly guaranteed (Article 6, GUMG). But this has a proviso: According to Article 18, paragraph 2, of the GUMG, the doctor must immediately inform the person concerned if he or she faces a direct physical danger that can be averted. The right to ignorance is not only granted to those persons whose gametes are being analysed – because certain test findings can also concern persons related by blood, since they allow certain conclusions to be drawn with regard to their gametes, Article 6 of the GUMG also grants these persons the right to decline information as pertains to their gametes (see *Botschaft* GUMG, 7399). Of course, it remains contested how this right can in actual fact be protected in a legal relationship governed by private law. The individual concerned can draw any conclusions he or she likes from the test's findings. Written consent is required for presymptomatic analyses.

495. Before and after they are undertaken, presymptomatic genetic analyses (which the law classifies as genetic tests that must be carried out before appearance of clinical symptoms, and with the aim of recognizing a certain predisposition for whatever malady) must be accompanied by a non-directive genetic briefing that encompasses more than just the usual pre-operative discussion (see *Botschaft* GUMG, 7414). The briefing must be documented. The briefing's frame of reference and the regulations that provide for a necessary waiting period are essentially the same as those for the genetic briefing accompanying prenatal genetic screenings. The law states that the most important points to be addressed in the conversation with the concerned party are information regarding the purpose, type, and conclusiveness of the test and the possibility of follow-up measures. The doctor is also required to provide information about any possible risk that might accompany the test, the frequency and type of disorder that might be diagnosed, any possible physical and mental strains, the meaning of the disorder, and the range of therapeutic or prophylactic measures on offer. The impacted individual must be instructed as to support possibilities and be counselled on the costs that might have to be borne as a result of the test and any possible follow-up measures.

496. Genetic analyses of mentally incompetent persons may only be carried out if they are necessary for the individual's health. An exception is when a serious congenital disorder in the family or a corresponding predisposition cannot be otherwise clarified and the burden to the individual concerned (e.g., through a saliva or blood sample) is minimal (Article 10, paragraph 2, GUMG). Within these limits, the legal representative of a mentally incompetent person is responsible for deciding whether any such genetic test should be allowed.

§5. Psycho-Surgical Interventions

497. In Switzerland, there are no special regulations for psycho-surgical measures – i.e., for brain operations undertaken to treat psychiatric afflictions or disorders. This means that the general principles applying to curative treatments hold here as well. According to these, in every case, the mentally competent patient must give his or her consent; if the patient is not competent, the legal representative's consent is required. If the mentally incompetent patient is likely to (re)obtain competency at a later date, then the procedure must be deferred insofar as this is medically possible. In the case of incompetent patients, the basic principle is that the legal representative may only give his or her consent to those procedures that are in the immediate self-interest of the patient – i.e., a procedure from which the patient can expect to obtain personal benefit. The prerequisite for the permissibility of a certain psycho-surgical measure carried out on incompetent patients might also be that less drastic measures or measures that have proven successful are unavailable and that the envisaged treatment can be expected to effect a cure. Individual treatments on permanently incompetent patients are only permissible in this area if the patient is greatly suffering and if no other or further treatments are available. The research done on incompetent patients is subject to special provisions.

§6. Organ Transplants

I. Constitutional Principles

498. Article 119a of the Swiss Federal Constitution grants the federal government comprehensive powers to regulate, in every regard, the transplantation of organs, tissues, and cells of human and animal origin (see *Botschaft Transplantationsgesetz*, 67). In doing so, the federal government must protect personality rights, health, and human dignity. In view of the well-known scarcity of organs, the federal government has been entrusted with the task of establishing criteria for an equitable allocation of organs. In order to curb the commercialization of the human body, the constitution has prohibited the traffic in human organs and has forbidden monetary remuneration for human organs, tissues, and cells. Transplantations must be based on the idea of solidarity and not on financial incentive. The aforementioned constitutional provisions are directly applicable to private individuals and create direct obligations for them as well. From a constitutional standpoint, on the other hand, the trade in human tissues and cells and animal organs is permissible – with the exception of human germ cells and embryonic products (Article 119, paragraph 2e, BV). Not subject to the commercial prohibition is reimbursement of the donor for any costs incurred.

II. Federal Law on the Transplantation of Organs, Tissues, and Cells

A. Content, Aim, and Principles of the Law

499. The *Bundesgesetz über die Transplantation von Organen, Geweben und Zellen* (*Transplantationsgesetz*, Federal Law on the Transplantation of Organs, Tissues and Cells) came into force on 1 July 2007. Diverse implementing regulations went into effect at the same time, each governing certain special areas in detail – the Transplantation Ordinance, the Organ Allocation Ordinance, and, building upon that, the Organ Allocation Ordinance of the Federal Department of the Interior (EDI), the Xenotransplantation Ordinance, and the Transplantation Fee Ordinance.

500. The Transplantation Law dictates the conditions under which organs, tissues, or cells can be used for purposes of transplantation, attempts to thwart misuses, and endeavours to guarantee personality rights and an individual's health and human dignity (Article 1, *Transplantationsgesetz*). The law covers organs, tissues, and cells of human or animal origin, as well as the products fashioned therefrom – but not artificially manufactured or devitalized products (e.g., artificial heart valves), blood and blood products (with the exception of blood stem cells), gametes, impregnated ova, or embryos. There are special legal regulations for each of these substances and products not falling within the scope of this law.

501. The Transplantation Law contains separate provisions on human and animal organs, tissues, and cells as well as transplantation products, this latter being understood by the law as products manufactured from human or animal organs, tissues, or cells in a standardized process (Article 3d, *Transplantationsgesetz*). In principle, the same provisions as for biological pharmaceuticals apply to transplantation products (Article 49, *Transplantationsgesetz*; see also *Botschaft Transplantationsgesetz*, 138 et seq.). Along with the Transplantation Law, certain provisions of the *Heilmittelgesetz* (Pharmaceuticals Law) are applicable to transplantation products (Article 49, *Transplantationsgesetz*). The Transplantation Law details the constitutional principles of the prohibition on commerce with human organs, tissues, and cells as well as the non-remuneration for donors (Articles 6 and 7, *Transplantationsgesetz*). These principles hold for living and deceased donors. Organs, tissues, and cells as such may not be sold (*Botschaft Transplantationsgesetz*, 137). It is thus forbidden to give or receive any financial or other advantage from a donation. The prohibition covers every form of monetary compensation, including payment in kind or other benefits. Permissible, however, is reimbursement for lost income, the costs of medical treatment, damages directly arising from the extraction from the donor, and retroactive symbolic gestures of gratitude. Crossover transplantation is also permitted.

502. The interdiction on commerce encompasses the trade in human organs, tissues, and cells within Switzerland and from Switzerland to foreign countries. The notion of 'trade' presupposes that the activity entails pursuit of one's own (material) advantage (*Botschaft Transplantationsgesetz*, 138). It is moreover forbidden to extract or transplant human organs, tissues, or cells that have been acquired for money or the securing of advantages. But the prohibition on trade has no application in terms of the reimbursement of costs incurred in connection with the transplantation, for instance, in the extraction or transport of organs, tissues, or cells. Furthermore, the trade in transplantation products – i.e., organs, tissues, or cells that are processed in a standardized way – is explicitly excluded from the trade prohibition.

B. Extraction of Transplants from Deceased Persons

503. In conformity with the constitutional provisions on the protection of personality rights and the individual's health and human dignity, Article 8 of the Transplantation Law contains the expanded assent solution ('*Zustimmungslösung*'). This best guarantees the donor's right to self-determination. Along with confirmation of the donor's death, the precondition for extracting a person's organs, tissues, or cells is the deceased person's prior consent to such an operation (Article 8, paragraph 1, *Transplantationsgesetz*). If there is no documented declaration of the deceased person's desires, his or her nearest relatives are asked whether they are aware of any declaration regarding the donation, which (whether consent or refusal) would take precedence over the desires of the relatives, whose decisions are subordinate to those of the deceased (Article 8, paragraphs 2 and 5, *Transplantationsgesetz*). If the deceased did not address the question of donation during his or her lifetime, then organs, tissues, and cells can only be extracted under the condition that the closest relatives agree to the donation; but their decision is bound by the presumed desire of the deceased (Article 8, paragraph 3, *Transplantationsgesetz*). If no close relatives can be contacted, extraction is impermissible. If during his or her lifetime the deceased confided the decision regarding donation to a trusted person, then this latter stands in for the relatives (Article 8, paragraph 6, *Transplantationsgesetz*). A person is authorized to render a declaration regarding donation at the age of 16 (Article 8, paragraph 7, *Transplantationsgesetz*).

504. As criterion for the confirmation of death, the Transplantation Law invokes the 'brain-death concept', which will not be expressly regulated in Swiss law until a law to that effect comes into force, but which still accords with accepted practice. According to this concept, a person is judged to be legally dead after the irreversible loss of cerebral functions, including that of the brainstem (Article 9, *Transplantationsgesetz*). Due to their extremely technical nature and frequent need to be adapted, the exact provisions regarding the confirmation of death are contained in the Transplantation Ordinance. This allows the provisions to be more quickly adapted to changed perceptions and medical advances than would be the case if they were enshrined in law in the formal sense. On the other hand, the independence of physicians is laid down in the Transplantation Law (Article 11): Doctors who are charged with confirming death may not help perform the extraction or transplantation and may not be subordinate to the orders of those who are undertaking such measures. These provisions are intended to preclude dependencies within the hospital hierarchy (*Botschaft Transplantationsgesetz*, 144).

505. Medical measures that serve the sole purpose of preserving organs, tissues, or cells in dying donors may only be implemented under the condition that the donor has given his or her free and informed consent to such measures, which are in every case prohibited if they could accelerate the donor's death or lead to a permanent vegetative state (Article 10, *Transplantationsgesetz*).

506. The Transplantation Law is currently under partial revision, which *inter alia* concerns its Article 8 regulating the preconditions for removal of organs from a deceased person and Article 10 on preparatory medical measures.

507. The amended Article 8 of the Transplantation Law provides that if no documented consent or refusal by the deceased person is available, the relatives must be asked whether they are aware of the person concerned having declared an intention to donate. If they are not aware of any such declaration, organs, tissues or cells may be removed if they consent to the removal. Before the amendment of the law, it was uncertain whether such request can be made only after the death of the person concerned has been confirmed or already before. This is especially crucial with regard to so-called non-heart-beating-donors: If the time span between asystole due to breaking off life-sustaining measures and brain-death is longer than sixty minutes, the risk of damaged organs is so high that transplantation is no longer medically indicated. Therefore, the amended Transplantation Law provides that the request can be made as soon as life-sustaining measures have been broken off. It must not be awaited until the brain-death is confirmed.

508. Article 10 of the Transplantation Law on preparatory medical measures provides that medical measures intended solely to preserve organs, tissues, or cells may only be undertaken prior to the death of the patient if the patient has been informed comprehensively and has freely given consent. Such measures are, however, prohibited if they hasten the death of the patient or may lead to the patient entering a permanent vegetative state. If the patient has not declared his or her intention of donating, such measures may be carried out after the death of the patient until the next of kin have reached a decision. There former Article 10 of the Transplantation Law provided no representation rules with regard to preparatory medical measures before the confirmed death of the patient.

509. The amended Transplantation Law adopts a provision in this respect. It allows for a representation by the next of kin in case the patient has not declared his or her intention with regard to the preparatory medical measures. The representatives have to decide according to the patient's presumed will. If the presumed will of the patient cannot be determined, the representatives can agree to the preparatory medical measures, if these are necessary for a successful transplantation of organs, tissues, or cells and if they only impose minimal risks and burden on the donor. However, consent is only possible after the decision to break off the life-sustaining measures has been taken. If the donating patient is incompetent and there are no next of kin, or they cannot be contacted, preparatory medical measures remain prohibited.

C. Extraction of Transplants from Living Persons

510. In principle, according to Article 12 of the Transplantation Law living organ donation is only permissible in the case of individuals who are mentally competent and have reached the age of majority (i.e., at least 18 years of age). In addition, the individuals must provide their free, written, and fully informed consent. Further conditions for the permissibility of such donation are the absence of any serious risk to the life or health of the donor as well as the absence of another therapeutic method of comparable benefit for the recipient. A personal or even familial relationship with the recipient is not a condition for the permissibility of a living donation.

511. In principle, persons who are mentally incompetent or under the age of majority cannot have their organs, tissues, or cells extracted (Article 13, *Transplantationsgesetz*). However, the law provides for exceptions: Reclaimable tissues or cells (but not organs) may be extracted if the extraction carries only a minimal risk and burden for the incompetent or underage donor and no suitable person who is competent or of age can be found. Additionally, the donation must be of a lifesaving nature and its recipient must be a parent, child, or sibling of the donor who is incompetent or under age. If the donor is under age yet competent, he or she must give free, written, and fully informed consent to the extraction. In the case of incompetent persons, the extraction is permissible under the condition that there is no indication that they would oppose any extraction. The scope of this provision, which resembles a veto power, is currently unclear, in particular because there is no further clarification of how clearly and on what occasions refusal must be expressed. In the view of the legislators, the refusal of donation on the part of an incompetent person must be respected in all cases (*Botschaft Transplantationsgesetz*, 146 et seq.). Even incompetent persons must be involved in the informational and consensual process as far as possible, and a further requirement is the written consent of the legal representative and an independent authority determined by the canton.

512. As a supplement to the *Sozialversicherungsrecht* (Social Insurance Law), the Transplantation Law also regulates the main features of insurance coverage for living donors (Article 14, *Transplantationsgesetz*). The donor must be appropriately insured against any serious consequences of the extraction.

D. Allocation of Organs

513. Moreover, the Transplantation Law regulates the handling of organs that are not donated to a certain designated person. The allocation of donated organs is centrally coordinated by a national allocation office, namely Swisstransplant, the Swiss Foundation for Organ Donations. It maintains a waiting list for all of Switzerland and allocates the organs to recipients after conferring with the various transplantation centres. The principle of non-discrimination is of utmost importance in the allocation of the organs (Article 17, *Transplantationsgesetz*): No one may be discriminated against in this process. Swiss residents must receive equal treatment.

Non-residents who have been placed on the waiting list can only receive an organ under certain conditions – a restriction intended to head off any 'transplantation tourism' (see *Botschaft Transplantationsgesetz*, 149). According to the Transplantation Law, the most important criteria for the allocation of organs are medical urgency, medical benefit, the period of time that someone has been waiting for an organ, and equal opportunity (Article 18, *Transplantationsgesetz*). No allowance is made for a person experiencing social hardship, for example, a person who has a possible obligation to care for underage children (*Botschaft Transplantationsgesetz*, 149 et seq.). The criterion of equal opportunity is intended to create a level playing field for patients with certain disadvantages (e.g., a rare blood type). Regulations for the weighting and ordering of the criteria for allocating organs are left to the Federal Council, which has met its obligations in this regard by enacting two ordinances, the *Organzuteilungsverordnung* (Organ Allocation Ordinance) and the *Organzuteilungsverordnung* EDI (Organ Allocation EDI).

E. Authorization, Duty to Report and Duty of Care

514. The Transplantation Law presupposes consent for the transplantation of organs (Article 27, *Transplantationsgesetz*) and thus ensures the quality of the transplantation and protection of its recipient. Furthermore, there is a reporting duty not only for the extraction of organs, tissues, or cells (Article 24, *Transplantationsgesetz*), but also for the transplantation of tissues or cells (Article 29, *Transplantationsgesetz*). Its objective is to protect the population from abuses and to ensure efficient oversight (see *Botschaft Transplantationsgesetz*, 157). The law also imposes a duty to exercise due care with regard to the extraction and transplantation of organs, tissues, or cells, for example, the obligation to test the transplants for pathogenic agents (Articles 30 et seq., *Transplantationsgesetz*). Those persons who have already received xenotransplants are precluded from donating. Furthermore, the transplant must be properly identifiable at all times and traceable back to the donor or recipient.

F. Human Embryonic or Foetal Tissues and Cells

515. Because human embryonic or foetal tissues and cells used for transplantations normally stem from abortions, Article 37, paragraph 1, of the Transplantation Law lays down the principle that the point in time and the method of the abortion must be chosen independently of any later transplantation, and the choice of method must be solely based on the woman's welfare (*Botschaft Transplantationsgesetz*, 161). The law also forbids in its Article 37, paragraph 2, certain practices: After the seventh day of their development, surplus embryos or aborted embryos and foetuses may not be kept artificially alive for the purpose of extracting their tissues or cells for transplantation; however, the preservation or multiplication of individual cells or tissues is permitted (see *Botschaft Transplantationsgesetz*, 161). In order to prevent abuse, embryonic and foetal cells or tissues intended for particular recipients are impermissible; that is, the donor may not designate a person in whom the cells or tissues of the embryo or foetus are to be transplanted. Moreover, it is forbidden to employ embryonic or foetal cells for purposes of transplantation if they are from mentally incompetent women (Article 37, paragraph 2 c, *Transplantationsgesetz*).

516. Only after a woman has decided to have an abortion may she be asked if tissues or cells from the aborted embryo or foetus can be employed for purposes of transplantation (Article 39, paragraph 1, *Transplantationsgesetz*). This is intended to prevent false incentives for an abortion and any kind of pressure being applied to the woman. Cells and tissue of an aborted foetus or embryo may only be used for purposes of transplantation if the donor freely gives her written and fully informed consent (Article 39, paragraph 2, *Transplantationsgesetz*). A similar regulation holds for surplus embryos: The couple may only be asked if cells or tissues from the embryo may be used for purposes of transplantation after it has been established that there are surplus embryos (Article 40, paragraph 1, *Transplantationsgesetz*). The use of tissues or cells from embryos for purposes of transplantation is only permissible if the couple concerned freely gives their fully informed and written consent (Article 40, paragraph 2, *Transplantationsgesetz*). In order to prevent any possible influences, there must be a separation between the persons participating in the transplantation and those who are undertaking an abortion or taking part in the reproductive process. There may also be no influence exerted one way or the other, and certainly no orders given (Article 41, *Transplantationsgesetz*).

517. There is no provision in the Transplantation Law stating that the death of the embryo or foetus must be confirmed before extraction of tissues or cells. It might be the case that at the time of extraction the aborted foetus – according to the conceptual principles of cerebral death – is still alive.

518. In standard therapies and clinical experiments, the transplantation of human embryonic tissues, foetal tissues, or cells to humans requires free consent (Article 38, *Transplantationsgesetz*).

G. Xenotransplantation

519. With an eye to the related high risk of infection, the Transplantation Law requires authorization of the transplantation of animal organs, tissues, or cells (or those transplantation products manufactured from them) to humans (Article 43, *Transplantationsgesetz*). Xenotransplantation is only permissible under certain conditions. Particularly critical in this regard are the therapeutic benefits and safety with respect to the risk of infection for the population. Recipients of xenotransplants are subject to especially careful monitoring with regard to pathogens, which includes a post-mortem examination (Article 44, *Transplantationsgesetz*). This lifelong after-care must be ensured by those persons holding an authorization to perform a xenotransplantation, thus allowing for early detection of zoonoses and a minimizing of danger for the population. If a case arises in which the population's security could be threatened, all necessary countermeasures must be taken immediately and the responsible authorities notified. Furthermore, the Transplantation Law contains provisions on holding individuals liable for possible zoonoses (Article 47, *Transplantationsgesetz*). Further provisions addressing xenotransplantation are contained in the *Verordnung des Bundesrates über die Transplantation von tierischen Organen, Geweben oder Zellen* (Ordinance of the Federal Council on the Transplantation of Animal Organs, Tissues or Cells [Xenotransplantation Ordinance]).

III. The Council of Europe's Additional Protocol concerning the Transplantation of Human Organs and Tissues

520. On 11 July 2002, Switzerland signed the Council of Europe's Additional Protocol to the Convention on Human Rights and Biomedicine concerning Transplantation of Organs and Tissues of Human Origin. The Additional Protocol, which went into force on 1 May 2006, not only stipulates a minimum international standard of protection with regard to the transplantation of human organs and tissues, but also constitutes an important transnational instrument for preventing the trade in organs.

521. On 12 June 2009, the parliament approved the Additional Protocol; it entered into force on 1 March 2010.

522. There are three ways in which the Swiss Transplantation Law adopts a more liberal attitude towards living donor transplantation than the Additional Protocol. First, in contrast to Article 9 of the Additional Protocol, the Swiss Transplantation Law does not stipulate a subsidiary status to living donor transplantation but allows for this option to be a primary therapy – particularly as one can expect better results from it than from transplanting the organs and tissues of a deceased person. Thus, in contrast to Article 14 of the Additional Protocol, the Swiss Transplantation Law allows for living donor transplantation of reclaimable tissues and cells (though not organs) from mentally incompetent individuals not only for the benefit of siblings but also parents or children. In the end, the Swiss Transplantation Law eschews the condition in Article 10 of the Additional Protocol, which stipulates that in any living donor transplantation, there must be a close personal relationship between the recipient and the donor; or, if such is lacking, there must be approval by an independent authority. But according to both the Swiss Transplantation Law and Article 10 of the Transplantation Ordinance, an experienced and independent expert must verify that any consent to a living transplantation is given freely and without financial incentives. Upon ratification of the Additional Protocol, corresponding provisos were attached to the three aforementioned aspects of living transplantations – provisos that are of course partially identical to those provisos already attached to ratification of the Biomedicine Convention.

§7. EXPERIMENTS ON HUMAN BEINGS

I. The Legal Foundations of Research on Human Beings

523. Articles 15 et seq. of the Biomedicine Convention regulate scientific research on human beings and embryos in the field of biology and medicine. The Additional Protocol Concerning Biomedical Research (2005), which has not been yet ratified in Switzerland, specifies the requirements. Because of Switzerland's monistic tradition, the norms of the Biomedicine Convention that are sufficiently defined and grant the individual certain rights with respect to the state are self-executing and accordingly need no adaptation to national law. Court rulings and legal doctrine will have to precisely clarify which norms in the Biomedicine Convention are applicable. The Biomedicine Convention contains numerous provisions addressing research carried out on humans and defines a minimum standard for the protection of human rights in medical research.

524. Switzerland has recently enacted a comprehensive statute in the area of research on humans. Until the HFG entered into force on 1 January 2014, protection of individuals against infringement of personal rights in the context of scientific research followed primarily from general provisions on personality protection in conjunction with relevant specific laws. Different provisions of the Swiss Federal Constitution guaranteed protection of personality rights with regard to researchers at public institutions. The ZGB guaranteed protection of personality rights vis-à-vis private researchers in a general way in Articles 27 et seq. Also applicable to medical research were, in particular, the *Stammzellenforschungsgesetz* (StFG, Stem Cell Research Law), the *Fortpflanzungsmedizingesetz* (FMedG, Reproductive Health Law), the *Transplantationsgesetz* (Transplantation Law), and the *Bundesgesetz über genetische Untersuchungen beim Menschen* (GUMG, Federal Law on Genetic Research Tests on Humans). The *Bundesgesetz über Arzneimittel und Medizinprodukte* (HMG, Federal Law on Pharmaceuticals and Medical Devices) was authoritative for clinical experiments with medicinal substances.

525. Apart from that, regulation of research on humans has traditionally fallen within the jurisdiction of the cantons, but regulations differed considerably from one canton to the next, in part with respect to their scope, content, and degree of detail.

526. Since the referendum on 7 March 2010, Article 118b of the Swiss Federal Constitution provides guidelines at the constitutional level for research on humans and vests the Swiss federal government with comprehensive powers to issue conclusive provisions in this area. Thereby, it must preserve the freedom to conduct research and must take into account the importance of research for society (Article 118b, paragraph 1, BV). Participation in research on humans requires an informed consent (Article 118b, paragraph 2 a, BV). Participants can revoke their consent at any time. Further, the risks for physical and mental integrity of the participants must not be disproportionate to the benefits of the research project (Article 118b, paragraph 2 b, BV). The interests of the participants take precedence over the interests of science and society. Hence, Article 118b, paragraph 2 b of the

Swiss Federal Constitution specifies the principle of proportionality (Article 5, paragraph 2, BV) in the context of research on human beings. It prohibits putting individuals at unnecessary risk. Research on humans can only take place if comparable results cannot be achieved by means of alternative research methods ('principle of subsidiarity') and if the research project's expected benefit outweighs the associated risks to the physical and mental integrity of the test person ('principle of benefit-risk analysis'). An independent institution must assess the compatibility of each research project with the above-stated principles (Article 118b, paragraph 2 d, BV).

527. The HFG entered into force on 1 January 2014 and applies to research about diseases, and the structure and functioning of the human body. Ethical, scientific and legal requirements are specified in the Ordinance on Clinical Trials in Human Research (Clinical Trials Ordinance; ClinO), the Ordinance on Human Research with the Exception of Clinical Trials (Human Research Ordinance, HRO) and the Ordinance on Organisational Aspects of the Law on Research on Human Beings (HRL Organisation Ordinance, OrgO-HRL). The ordinances also entered into force on 1 January 2014. The Clinical Trials Ordinance regulates research projects which fall within the definition of clinical trials according to Article 3 l of the HFG, i.e., research projects in which persons are prospectively assigned to a health-related intervention in order to investigate its effects on health or on the structure and functioning of the human body. The Human Research Ordinance regulates human research projects with the exception of clinical trials; and the authorization and notification procedures for these research projects. The Organisation Ordinance regulates the organization of the research ethics commissions. The implementation of the HFG and of associated ordinances lies within the responsibility of cantonal ethics commissions, the Swiss Agency for Therapeutic Products (Swissmedic) and competent federal authorities (Federal Health Office, Federal Environment Office).

528. The Guideline for Good Clinical Practice of the International Conference on Harmonization (1996) is also applicable in Switzerland. It encompasses international ethical and scientific quality standards for designing, conducting, recording, and reporting trials of pharmaceutical products that involve the participation of human subjects. Article 5, paragraph 1, annex 1, no. 2.1 of the Clinical Trials Ordinance refers to the Guideline for Good Clinical Practice.

II. HFG: Purpose and Scope of Its Application

529. The purpose of the HFG is to protect the dignity, privacy and health of human beings involved in research (Article 1, paragraph 1, HFG). It applies to research concerning human diseases and the structure and functioning of the human body, which involves persons, deceased persons, embryos and foetuses, biological material, and health-related personal data (Article 2, paragraph 1, HFG). The HFG, however, does not apply to research which involves embryos in vitro (this falls within the scope of the StFG), anonymized biological material and anonymously collected or anonymized health-related data (Article 2, paragraph 2, HFG).

III. General Principles Governing Research on Living Human Beings

530. In its second section, the HFG provides general principles which are applicable in all areas of research on human beings (Articles 4 et seq., HFG). In accordance with Article 118b, paragraph 2 b, and Article 5, paragraph 2, of the Swiss Federal Constitution, Article 4, of the HFG states that interests, health and welfare of the individual human being must prevail over the interests of science and society. In order to accentuate the precedence of individual interests over public interests, research involving human beings may only be carried out if the persons concerned after being duly informed have given their consent (Article 7, HFG; 'principle of informed consent'). The interests of the participants are further protected by the prohibition of discrimination (Article 6, HFG) and the right to be informed about results relating to his or her health and all the personal data (Article 8, HFG). According to the former principle, no group of people shall be disproportionately included in or excluded from research without good reason.

531. The HFG also lays down principles aiming at protecting the integrity and public image of research involving human beings. Research involving human beings may therefore only be carried out if it addresses a topic of scientific relevance concerning the understanding of human diseases, the structure and functioning of the human body or public health (Article 5, HFG). Research involving human beings must further comply with the generally recognized scientific requirements (Article 10, HFG), in particular scientific integrity and quality, and appropriate professional qualifications of the involved persons. Finally, the commercialization of research on human beings is prohibited. According to Article 9 of the HFG, the human body or parts thereof may not be disposed of or acquired as such for research purposes in return for payment or other non-cash advantage. This provision protects the human dignity and integrity. Indeed, financial incentives could result in test persons underestimating or accepting unreasonable risks.

IV. Research Involving Competent Persons of Full Age

532. The HFG statutorily embeds the principle of subsidiarity (Article 11, HFG) and the principle of benefit-risk analysis (Article 12, HFG). Research on humans can only take place if comparable results cannot be achieved by means of alternative research methods and if the research project's expected benefit outweighs the potential risks to the physical and mental integrity of the participant. Article 12, paragraph 1, of the HFG specifies the bioethical principle of *neminem laedere*: the risks and burdens have to be minimized as far as possible. Therefore, anyone conducting a research project must take all the measures required to protect the participants (Article 15, paragraph 1, HFG). If, during the research project, circumstances arise which could jeopardize the safety or health of the participants or lead to a disproportionate relationship between the risks and burdens and the benefits, all the measures required to ensure protection are to be taken without delay (Article 15, paragraph 2, HFG). There is a liability of the person conducting the project for damages to the participants (Article 19, HFG).

533. Persons may only be involved in a research project if they have given their informed consent in writing (Article 16, paragraph 1, HFG). According to Article 16, paragraph 2, of the HFG, the briefing is only complete if the person concerned received oral and written information on the nature, purpose, duration and procedure of the research project (a), the foreseeable risks and burdens (b), the expected benefits of the research project, in particular for themselves or for other people (c), the measures taken to protect the personal data collected (d), and their rights (e). In exceptional cases, the persons concerned may be given incomplete information regarding individual aspects of a research project, insofar as this is essential for methodological reasons and if the research project entails no more than minimal risks and burdens (Article 18, paragraph 1, HFG). The Clinical Trials Ordinance and the Human Research Ordinance formulate additional requirements with regard to the briefing.

534. The person concerned may withhold or revoke his or her consent at any time, and without giving any reason (Article 7, paragraph 2, HFG).

535. The consent must refer to a particular research project. The use of biological material and health-related personal data obtained in the course of a project for other or future research is prohibited. Exceptions to this principle are regulated in Articles 31–34 of the HFG.

536. For reasons of protection of test persons in research projects with an expected direct benefit, the use of a placebo or non-treatment is only permissible if no additional risk of serious or irreversible harm is to be expected and no standard treatment is available, or if the use of a placebo is required for compelling, scientifically sound methodological reasons, in order to establish the efficacy or safety of a treatment method (Article 13, HFG).

537. Furthermore, Article 14 of the HFG specifies the prohibition of commercialization as laid down in its Article 9. Accordingly, no person may receive payment or any other non-cash advantage for participating in a research project with an expected direct benefit. Participation in a research project with no expected direct benefit may be appropriately remunerated (Article 14, paragraph 1, HFG). No person may demand or accept payment or any other non-cash advantage from another in return for the latter's participation in a research project (Article 14, paragraph 2, HFG).

V. Research Involving Children, Adolescents, and Incompetent Adults

538. The HFG provides additional requirements for research involving particularly vulnerable persons. Regarding research involving children, the law differentiates between research projects with direct benefit and research projects with indirect benefit, and whether the child concerned has power of judgment or not. Incompetent children, adolescents and adults must be involved as much as possible in the consent procedure (Article 21, paragraph 1, HFG). The older incompetent children and adolescents are, the bigger the weight that has to be accorded to their views (Article 21, paragraph 2, HFG). In the context of the HFG, a child is a legal minor if he has not reached the age of 14 years yet (Article 3 j, HFG). Adolescents are legal minors aged 14 years or more (Article 3 k, HFG).

539. A research project with an expected direct benefit may only be carried out on competent children if the child and his or her legal representative have given the informed consent in writing (Article 22, paragraph 1, HFG). A research project with no expected direct benefit may only be carried out on competent children if, in addition to the aforementioned consent, it entails no more than minimal risks and burdens and it can be expected to yield substantial findings which could in the long term be beneficial for persons with the same disease or disorder, or in the same situation (Article 22, paragraph 2, HFG). A research project with an expected direct benefit may only be carried out on incompetent children if the legal representative has given informed consent in writing and the child does not visibly oppose to the research intervention either verbally or by his or her behaviour (Article 22, paragraph 3, HFG). A research project with no expected direct benefit may only be carried out on incompetent children if it entails no more than minimal risks and burdens and it can be expected to yield substantial findings which could in the long term be beneficial for persons with the same disease or disorder, or in the same situation, the legal representative has given informed consent in writing and the child does not visibly oppose to the research intervention either verbally or by his or her behaviour (Article 22, paragraph 4, HFG).

540. Research involving adolescents must meet the same requirements as research involving children (Article 23, HFG). However, in the case of research on competent adolescent, the informed consent of the parents does not have to be given if the research project entails only minimal risks and burdens (Article 23, paragraph 1 b, HFG).

541. A research project with an expected direct benefit may only be carried out on incompetent adults if the person concerned gave his or her consent while in a state of capacity and this is duly documented. If no documented consent is available, the research may also be carried out if an informed consent has been given in writing by the legal representative, a designated trusted person or the next of kin, and the test person does not visibly express opposition to the research intervention either verbally or by his or her behaviour (Article 24, paragraph 1, HFG). A research project with no expected direct benefit may only be carried out on incompetent adults if, in addition to the aforementioned requirements, it entails no more than minimal risks and burdens and it can be expected to yield substantial findings which could in the long term be beneficial for persons with the same disease or disorder, or in the same situation (Article 24, paragraph 2, HFG).

VI. Research Involving Pregnant Women and Embryos and Foetuses In Vivo

542. Article 25 of the HFG proscribes research projects designed to modify properties of an embryo or foetus for non-disease-related reasons. Human enhancement and research in this field are generally banned.

543. Research with permissible objectives must consider Article 26 of the HFG. The provision distinguishes between research projects with a direct benefit for the woman concerned or for an embryo or foetus, and those without a direct benefit. They may only be carried out if the foreseeable risks and burdens, both for the pregnant woman and for the embryo or foetus, are not disproportionate to the expected benefits (Article 26, paragraph 1, HFG). A research project with no expected direct benefit for the pregnant woman or for the embryo or foetus may only be carried out if it entails no more than minimal risks and burdens for the embryo or foetus and it can be expected to yield substantial findings which could in the long term be beneficial for pregnant women or for embryos or foetuses (Article 26, paragraph 2, HFG). Furthermore, the pregnant woman involved must give her informed consent in writing (Article 16, paragraph 1, HFG). If the research project concerns methods of abortion, a pregnant woman may only be asked whether she wishes to participate in a research project after she has decided to undergo an abortion (Article 27, paragraph 1, HFG). While in these cases risks and burdens for the foetus are irrelevant, in respect to the pregnant woman the general rules on benefit-risk analysis apply (Article 12, HFG).

VII. Research Involving Prisoners

544. Imprisonment establishes a relationship of dependency between the prisoner and the state which operates the imprisonment institution. In order to safeguard the autonomy of the prisoner, his or her participation in a research project cannot be rewarded with special imprisonment conditions (Article 29, HFG). For reasons of protection of the physical and mental integrity, a research project with no expected direct benefit which involves prisoners may only be carried out if it entails no more than minimal risks and burdens (Article 28, paragraph 2, HFG). However, for research projects with an expected direct benefit which involve prisoners, the general requirements apply (Article 28, paragraph 1, HFG). In this case, research involving prisoners is not subsidiary to research involving other persons.

VIII. Research in Emergency Situations

545. In a case of emergency, in which the person concerned cannot validly consent due to incapacity, e.g., unconsciousness, Articles 30 et seq. of the HFG apply. A research project with an expected direct benefit may be carried out in emergency situations, if measures have been taken in order to determine the will of the person concerned as soon as possible, if the person concerned does not visibly oppose to the research intervention either verbally or by his or her behaviour, and if a doctor who is not participating in the research project is called in beforehand to safeguard the interests of the person concerned. In exceptional cases, where there are solid reasons for doing so, the doctor may be called in at a later stage (Article 30, paragraph 1, HFG). A research project with no expected direct benefit may be carried out in emergency situations if, in addition to the aforementioned requirements, it entails no more than minimal risks and burdens and it can be expected to yield substantial findings which could in the long term be beneficial for persons with the same disease or disorder, or in the same situation (Article 30, paragraph 2, HFG).

546. Both in case of a research project with an expected direct benefit and a research project with no expected direct benefit, the person concerned must be duly informed about the research project as soon as his or her conditions allows this (Article 31, paragraph 1, HFG). If the person concerned refuses to give his or her consent, the biological material and data obtained may no longer be used for the research project (Article 31, paragraph 2, HFG).

IX. Research Involving Deceased Persons

547. According to legal doctrine and the jurisprudence of the courts, anyone can validly determine how he or she is to be buried and what is to be done with his or her body (BGE 101 II 177, 190 et seq. [1975]). In order to best guarantee the donor's right to self-determination in the context of research on deceased persons, the HFG adopts the expanded assent solution ('*Zustimmungslösung*') of the Transplantation Law regulated in its Article 8 (cf. Article 36, paragraph 3, HFG). Research on deceased persons is permitted if he or she consented to the use of his or her body for research purposes during his or her lifetime (Article 36, paragraph 1, HFG). If no documented consent or refusal of the deceased person is available, the body or parts thereof may be used for research purposes if consent is given by the next of kin or by a trusted person designated during the lifetime of the deceased person (Article 36, paragraph 1, HFG). Only if the death of the person dates back more than seventy years, research can be carried out without the expanded assent. However, the next of kin retains the right of veto (Article 36, paragraph 4, HFG).

548. A further exception to the principle that research on deceased persons depends on the consent of the person concerned during his or her lifetime or the consent of his or her next kin is laid down in Article 38 of the HFG. Small quantities of bodily substances removed in the course of an autopsy or transplantation may be anonymized for research purposes without consent, unless there is a documented objection to this by the deceased person.

549. Indeed, a research project may be carried out on a deceased person only after his or her death has been determined (Article 37, paragraph 1, HFG). In Switzerland, a person is declared dead if the functions of his or her brain, including the brain stem, have ceased irreversibly (Article 9, paragraph 1, *Transplantationsgesetz*). A research project on the deceased person's physiological functions which are maintained by artificial respiration and medication can only be carried out if equivalent findings cannot be obtained otherwise (Article 37, paragraph 2, HFG). Furthermore, the person conducting the research must be independent from the persons responsible for determining the death (Article 37, paragraph 2, HFG).

X. Research Involving Embryos and Foetuses from Induced Abortions and from Spontaneous Abortions Including Stillbirths

550. Alongside with research involving embryos and foetuses in vivo, the HFG also provides for rules on research projects involving embryos and foetuses from (induced) abortions and spontaneous abortions and stillborn (Article 39, paragraph 3, and Article 40, paragraph 2, HFG).

551. A research project involving embryos and foetuses from induced abortions is permitted if the woman concerned, after sufficient briefing, has given her written consent (Article 39, paragraph 1, HFG, Article 16 and Articles 22–24 HFG apply *mutatis mutandis*). Before giving her consent, the woman must be granted an appropriate waiting period. In order to protect the autonomy of the woman and the woman's physical integrity, Article 39, paragraph 2, of the HFG stipulates that the point in time and method of the abortion must be chosen independently from the research project. Furthermore, the law stipulates that a pregnant woman may only be asked whether she wishes to place her foetus at the disposal of a research project after her decision to abort has been confirmed (Article 39, paragraph 1, HFG). This is to prevent the pregnant woman from being influenced in her decision by the possibility that the aborted foetus will be made available for research purposes. In order to ensure that these rules are observed and to avoid conflicts of interest, Article 39, paragraph 4, of the HFG provides that persons carrying out a research project with aborted embryos or foetuses may not be involved in the abortion and may not be authorized to give instructions to those persons participating in it.

552. A research project involving embryos and foetuses from spontaneous abortions and stillborn, presupposes the consent of the couple concerned (Article 40, paragraph 1, HFG); the requirements of the Article 16 of the HFG must be fulfilled.

XI. Further Use of Biological Material and Health-Related Personal Data for Research

553. Biological material (cells, tissue, body fluids, organs, etc.) can be obtained in numerous ways, for instance, through medically indicated extraction for purposes of diagnosis, or it can result from surgery (placenta, umbilical cord, etc.). Health-related personal data is mostly collected in the course of medical consultation. Biological material and health-related personal data can also be obtained and collected respectively for research purposes. There is a question under which circumstances biological material and personal data can be used for purposes outside of the scope of the medical intervention during which it was collected.

554. The HFG differentiates between biological material and genetic data on the one hand, and non-genetic health-related personal data on the other hand. Furthermore, the Law draws a distinction between uncoded, coded, and anonymized material and data.

555. Biological material and genetic data in a coded form may be used for research purposes if informed consent has been given by the person concerned, or by the legal representative or the next of kin (Article 32, paragraph 2, HFG and Articles 16 and 22–24, HFG apply *mutatis mutandis*). In the case of uncoded biological material and genetic data, informed consent of the person concerned or of the legal representative or the next of kin can only be given for the use in a particular, specified research project (Article 32, paragraph 1, HFG and Articles 16 and 22–24 HFG apply *mutatis mutandis*). Consenting to the general use in future research projects is not possible.

556. Non-genetic health-related personal data in an uncoded form can be used for research purposes if informed consent has been given by the person concerned, or by the legal representative or the next of kin (Article 33, paragraph 1, HFG and Articles 16 and 22–24, HFG apply *mutatis mutandis*). Coded non-genetic health-related personal data can be used for research purposes if the person concerned or the legal representative or the next of kin have been informed in advance and have not objected to the project (Article 33, paragraph 2, HFG and Articles 22–24, HFG apply *mutatis mutandis*).

557. The consent of the persons concerned to the use of biological material or personal data in research must be obtained at the time of extraction or collection (Article 17, HFG).

558. Biological material and genetic data may be anonymized for research purposes if the person concerned or the legal representative or the next of kin have been informed in advance and have not objected to the anonymization (Article 32, paragraph 3, HFG and Articles 22–24 HFG apply *mutatis mutandis*). Non-genetic health-related personal data, however, can be anonymized without presuppositions. The Federal Council has to specify the requirements for correct and secure anonymization and coding, and the conditions for breaking the code (Article 35, HFG). The HFG does not apply to anonymized biological material or anonymously collected or anonymized health-related data (Article 2, paragraph 2 b and c, HFG).

559. Article 34 of the HFG allows in certain defined cases for substitution of consent by ethics commissions. Biological material or health-related personal data may be used for research purposes in exceptional cases without consent if it is impossible or disproportionately difficult to obtain consent or to provide information on the right to object, or this would impose an undue burden on the person concerned (a); no documented objection is available (b); and the interests of research outweigh the interests of the person concerned in deciding on the use of his or her biological material and data (c).

560. Along with the use of biological material and health-related personal data, the HFG also regulates its transfer, export and storage (Articles 41 et seq., HFG).

561. In this context, it is noteworthy that the legislator abstained from specific regulations on biobanks. Biobanks are cryogenic storage facilities where human biological material is stored after its extraction.

XII. Supervision by Ethics Commissions

562. Ethics commissions are institutions pertaining to the cantonal public law (cf. Articles 51 et seq., HFG). They have to supervise research on human beings. Every research project on human beings has to be authorized by the responsible ethics commission (Article 45, paragraph 1 a, HFG). Authorization is granted if the ethical, legal, and scientific requirements of the HFG are met (Article 45, paragraph 2, HFG). If the safety or health of the persons concerned is at risk, the ethics commission may revoke or suspend its authorization or make the continuation of the research project subject to additional requirements (Article 48, paragraph 1, HFG). The ethics commission may request information or documentation from the holder of the authorization. This must be provided or made available free of charge (Article 48, paragraph 2, HFG).

563. The organization and proceedings of the ethics commissions, in particular the composition and the required qualification of their members, the proceedings and competences are regulated in the Organisation Ordinance to the HFG.

XIII. General Outline of the StFG

564. Research on embryos in vitro is prohibited in Switzerland; however, research on embryonic stem cells is allowed. The StFG, lays down the conditions under which human embryonic stem cells may be collected from surplus embryos and employed for research purposes (Article 1, paragraph 1, StFG). The law's scope is to prevent the incorrect handling of surplus embryos and embryonic stem cells and to protect human dignity (Article 1, paragraph 2, StFG).

565. To collect stem cells, one may only use embryos that have been produced in the course of in vitro fertilization, and that could not be inserted into the woman's uterus and thus have no chance of survival. When stem cells are extracted, the embryo must not be more than seven days old (Article 3, paragraph 1c, StFG). A surplus embryo may only be used to yield embryonic stem cells if the couple concerned has given their free and fully informed consent (Article 5, paragraph 1, StFG). The couple, or more precisely, the woman or the man, may revoke their consent at any time without stating their reason, until the stem cell extraction begins

(Article 5, paragraph 3, StFG). If consent is refused or revoked, the embryo must be destroyed immediately (Article 5, paragraph 4, StFG). To keep researchers from exerting pressure on the couple, Article 6 of the StFG stipulates, that persons attendant to the garnering of stem cells may neither be involved in the couple's reproductive process, nor have power to give instructions to individuals partaking in this process.

566. Persons who wish to garner embryonic stem cells from surplus embryos for purposes of a research project need authorization from the Federal Health Office. According to Article 7, paragraph 2, of the StFG, this authorization may be granted, if no suitable stem cells are available in the country (b); if no more surplus embryos are used than absolutely necessary for garnering embryonic stem cells (c); if the technical and operational conditions are fulfilled (d); and if the responsible ethics commission has screened and authorized it (a). According to Article 12 of the StFG, the ethics commission may only authorize the research project if its purpose is to acquire important knowledge on the detection, treatment, or prevention of serious diseases or on human developmental biology (a), and if equivalent findings cannot be obtained in any other way (b). Furthermore, the project must satisfy scientific quality requirements (c) and be ethically tenable in the view of the responsible ethics commission (d).

§8. Euthanasia

I. The Present Legal Situation

567. Up to now, there have been no special legal regulations in Switzerland treating the issue of assisted dying. The barriers to permissible assisted dying arise from the penal code, in particular from the section on homicide. For this reason, indirectly active and passive assisted dying are still permissible in Switzerland, whereas directly active assisted dying as an active killing of the patient by a third person (e.g., a doctor) who has the power to carry out the deed ('*Tatmacht*') is prohibited. The situation is different if the patient him- or herself takes a drug that has fatal effects but that the physician merely made available to the patient. In this case, from a legal standpoint, the patient commits a suicide in which the doctor and/or possible third persons provide assistance. Thus, according to the StGB, assisted suicide is not unlawful if it is not committed out of selfish motives (Article 115, StGB). From a European perspective, this is a liberal provision, and it is based on respect for the patient's autonomy. It is therefore permissible for the doctor to prescribe a fatal drug at request of the patient, who subsequently employs it so as to effect his or her wish to die. The most important precondition, however, is that the patient be mentally competent, which requires an especially careful scrutiny in view of the life-and-death decision involved. In order for assisted suicide to remain lawful, it is also absolutely necessary that the patient him- or herself have the power to carry out the deed. The patient must administer the fatal drug him- or herself; that is, he or she must swallow or inject it, or at least activate the infusion in which the drug is contained. If the patient is unable to do so owing to the afflicted condition (e.g., complete paralysis, inability to swallow, etc.) then suicide is no longer possible. If the drug is administered by a third person to the patient prepared to die, it becomes a case of impermissible active assisted dying. At least according to Article 114 of the StGB, the third party is liable to prosecution even if he or she administers the fatal drug – upon the patient's sincere and urgent request – out of estimable motives, e.g., pity.

568. In BGE 133 I 58 et seq. (2007), the Swiss Federal Supreme Court, as first signatory to the EHRC, explicitly acknowledged that the right of self-determination protected in Article 8, no. 1, of the EHRC contains the right 'to decide the time and manner of ending one's own life, at least if the person concerned is in a position to make up their own mind and act accordingly' (BGE 133 I 58, 67 [2007]; the so-called right to suicide). But it expressly denied that this provision or the protection of personal freedom (Article 10, paragraph 2, BV) could form the basis of a claim to suicide assistance from the state or third parties. In Switzerland, the right to suicide has long been acknowledged by prevailing legal opinion. The European Court of Human Rights (ECHR) confirmed the decision of the Swiss Federal Supreme Court in its judgment of 20 June 2011, Haas c. Switzerland, no. 31322/07.

569. From the standpoint of rules of conduct, the SAMW-*Richtlinien zur Betreuung von Patientinnen und Patienten am Lebensende* (SAMW Guidelines for the Care of Patients Close to Death, 2004, updated 2012) are premised on the permissibility of the prescription of a fatal drug by the doctor so long as the patient solicits it him- or herself and has a permanent wish to die. Along with the requirement that the patient is legally capable of giving consent, the guidelines contain further premises: The patient's ailment must justify the assumption that his or her death is near. Insofar as possible and desirable, alternatives must first be employed. Finally, the patient's desire to die must be closely scrutinized by an independent third party (SAMW-*Richtlinien zur Betreuung von Patientinnen und Patienten am Lebensende* [2004, updated 2012], no. 4.1, cf. SAMW- *Richtlinien zur Behandlung und Betreuung von älteren pflegebedürftigen Menschen* [2004, updated 2012], no. 6). If these conditions are fulfilled, the guidelines grant the doctor discretionary power to prescribe a fatal drug to the patient at the latter's request, but in no case is the doctor obligated to do so, as assisted suicide is not one of the physician's binding rules of conduct. The doctor can also refuse to prescribe a fatal agent by invoking his or her basic rights, in particular that of personal freedom (Article 10, paragraph 2, BV).

570. In its recent judgment of 14 May 2013, the European Court of Human Rights (ECHR) (*Gross v. Switzerland*, no. 67810/10) requested Switzerland to regulate the prescription of a fatal drug to the patient at the latter's request in a statutory law. In the particular case, an 80 years old woman submitted a request to the Health Board of the Canton of Zurich to be provided with 15 grams of sodium pentobarbital in order for her to commit suicide. She was no more willing to continue suffering the age-related decline of her physical and mental faculties. All the physicians approached declined to issue the requested prescription, as she was not suffering from a terminal illness. The cantonal authority denied her request as well. In its decision, the Court criticized that the access to a fatal drug was not regulated by statutory law, but only by a non-governmental organization. This resulted not only in legal uncertainty, but also was a source of a considerable degree of distress of the person concerned and therefore violated Article 8 of the EHRC. The Court acknowledged thereby that there might be difficulties in finding the necessary political consensus on such controversial questions with a profound ethical and moral impact. Nevertheless, the Court considered a statutory regulation inevitable.

571. However, the Grand Chamber of the European Court of Human Rights (ECHR), by nine against eight votes, declared on 30 September 2014 the case *Gross v. Switzerland* inadmissible on the grounds of abuse of the right of petition. The applicant ended her life on 10 November 2011, one year and a half earlier than the judgment of the European Court of Human Rights (ECHR).

II. Assisted Dying Organizations

572. In Switzerland, a variety of organizations under private law (the best known are EXIT and Dignitas) offer assisted suicide and work together with established physicians who prescribe the fatal drug to the patient. In connection with the activity of these organizations – and particularly in view of the fact that those persons without Swiss residency but after a short stay in Switzerland are also given death assistance by individual organizations – Switzerland has recently been confronted with the phenomenon of 'death tourism', in which persons from less liberal (in terms of suicide) neighbouring countries come to Switzerland for the specific purpose of being prescribed a fatal drug and dying. In order to curb this phenomenon, which has carried with it much negative media coverage in other parts of Europe, where some regard it as undignified, various political initiatives have been launched at the federal level to ban or regulate the activities of assisted dying organizations or at least to place them under government supervision (the Glanzmann Motion [2007] and also Stadler [2007]).

III. Revision of the Provisions on Assisted Dying

573. Creation of detailed regulations for assisted dying has been demanded on various occasions, including, in particular, a review of the prohibition on directly active assisted dying – the killing of someone who has freely elected to die at the hands of a third person (euthanasia). One example is the Ruffy Motion (1994), which parliament submitted in the form of a postulate to the Federal Council in 1996. Subsequently, the Federal Council commissioned an interdisciplinary committee with the task of clarifying whether questions impinging on assisted dying could and should be regulated by legislators. After two years of work, the committee's findings report of March 1999 essentially upheld the prohibition on directly active assisted dying while declaring that the creation of detailed provisions on indirectly active and passive assisted dying was necessary. Additionally, in extreme cases of directly active assisted dying, the possibility of an exemption from punishment was considered, although the fundamental unlawfulness of the act was not overturned. Despite the committee's proposals, no further concrete measures followed, and in 2000, Franco Cavalli, member of the National Council, established a parliamentary initiative to regulate active assisted dying in the spirit of the committee's proposal. Moreover, in March 2004, the Federal Assembly submitted the motion 'Assisted Dying and Palliative Care' to the *Kommission für Rechtsfragen des Ständerates* (Council of State's Commission for Legal Questions), which commissioned the Federal Council with drawing up a proposal for regulating indirectly active and passive assisted dying and formulating measures for furthering palliative care. In the following year, a motion was once again filed with the goal of requiring the Federal Council to advance work on the legal regulation of assisted dying and to supply parliament with a report on it.

574. Meanwhile, on 24 April 2006, the Swiss Justice and Police Department took a negative position on the plan to explicitly regulate assisted dying. It decided that the existing legal basis was sufficient for indirectly active and passive assisted dying. The uncertainty in these cases did not arise from the question of whether and when assisted dying should be allowed in principle, but rather from the question of who, in the case of a mentally incompetent patient, may and must decide (Federal Department of Justice and Police (EJPD), *Sterbehilfe*, 23). The department's view was that the prohibition on directly active assisted dying should be retained (EJPD, *Sterbehilfe*, 51). Subsequent to publication of the report, parliament's wish for legal regulation of assisted dying was again affirmed by means of a parliamentary initiative on the part of Christine Egerszegi-Obrist, member of the National Council.

575. In 2008, the Federal Council mandated the Department of Justice and Police to assess whether there is a need for a specific statutory regulation in this field. The Department introduced a preliminary draft including two alternatives for an amendment of Article 115 of the StGB. The first alternative provided for impunity for the responsible persons and members of assisted dying organizations under certain conditions. The second alternative imposed a total ban on assisted suicide. In the consultation process, both alternatives were highly controversial and no political consensus could be found. However, the majority of the participants in the consultation process argued in support of the need for legislative action in this field. Subsequently, in September 2010, the Federal Council mandated the Department of Justice and Police to revise the first alternative taking into account the results of the consultation.

576. On 29 March 2010, the Federal Health Office published the results of an extensive survey on assisted dying. According to the survey, a small majority opposes assisted dying. By contrast, a survey published by the Institute of Criminology of the University of Zurich the same year, came up with a very different result: a clear majority was in favour of assisted dying and stressed the right to self-determination of each person.

577. In its report of June 2011, the Federal Council came to the conclusion that an amendment of Article 115 of the StGB would lead to problems. Regulating the requirements of assisted dying would weaken the principle of sanctity of human life, would legitimize assisted dying organizations, and would inevitably still be a vague legal concept. In the end, specific legal regulation would not bring about any additional value. Therefore, the Federal Council opted against a revision of Article 115 of the Swiss Penal Code and for further promotion of palliative medicine and of measures to prevent suicide.

§9. Transsexuality and Intersexuality

578. There is currently no law governing transsexuality and intersexuality in Switzerland and none is in the planning. Only Article 7, paragraph 2 o, of the *Zivilstandsverordnung* (ZStV, Civil Status Ordinance) refers to sex change as a civil status which can be recorded in the register of births, marriages, and deaths. As a consequence, the general rules governing personal rights must be followed when judging the legality and the legal repercussions of sex-change and sex-assignment operations.

579. Sex-change operations on mentally competent transsexual persons are lawful if, after a comprehensive briefing, these persons give their consent to the medical procedure. If, following the operation, transsexual persons would like to have their sex change officially recognized by the state, they must institute legal proceedings with the relevant court to have their status changed in the register of births, marriages, and deaths (Article 42, ZGB). This will be approved if expert reports confirm that the sex change has in fact been effected and the ability to reproduce in the person's original sex has been precluded. In the interest of legal certainty, the Swiss Federal Supreme Court also requires expert confirmation of the sex-change operation's irreversibility (BGE 119 II 264, 270 [1993]). It should also be mentioned that an existing marriage does not hinder a change to an individual's status in the register and is not dissolved as a result of a change of sex in the register (according to a decision of the Bern Higher Court ['*Obergericht*'] from 29 July 2005, FamPra.ch 2006, 112 et seq.).

580. The legality of sex-assignment operations on mentally incompetent intersexual children has not been conclusively clarified. If one holds the view that intersexuality is an affliction and that the sex-assignment operation is necessary in order to cure the child, it is lawful, provided that the child's legal representatives give their fully informed consent. However, if one holds the view that such operations are merely of a cosmetic nature because intersexuality is not a medical condition, then the legal representatives of the incompetent child may not legally consent to the procedure, which is then prohibited. Upon attaining competency, the child can then decide for itself whether it approves the procedure or not.

581. In a recent, ground-breaking decision of 1 February 2011, the Zurich Higher Court ('*Obergericht*') discussed whether the official recognition of sex change by the state and accordingly the change of status in the register of births, marriages, and deaths, requires surgical measures and irreversible infertility. Former judicial practice required such surgical intervention. The Court reviewed this jurisprudence and decided that sex change is successfully completed when the person concerned identifies completely with the desired sex and is accepted as a member of that sex by others. This can also be achieved by means of hormonal treatment and further aesthetical measures and does not require surgery. Moreover, belonging to a particular gender is not determined by physical properties of a person only, but rather by his or her whole personality. A surgical intervention always carries a risk to the person's health and psychical stability. In this regard, the stringent requirement of a surgical intervention would mean a violation of the physical integrity. If the recognition of self-determined gender identity is made conditional upon a surgical intervention, a free decision with respect to the sex-change surgery is not available.

Part III. The Physician in Relation to the Healthcare System

Chapter 1. Collegial Relationships

§1. Associations

582. Although individual medical practices with a sole doctor in attendance are still frequently the norm, most newly established practices consist of medical groups in which a variety of doctors work together.

583. For the participating doctors, group practices have a variety of advantages and are also regarded as a model for the future in terms of healthcare economics. Among other things, administrative and organizational synergies can be created. In addition, doctors are not required to work the long hours that they might if they did not have colleagues helping to shoulder the extra burden. Such group offices also enable part-time work, which has become increasingly popular.

584. Up to now, most group practices have been structured as partnerships, which does not usually cause any licensing difficulties under cantonal law.

585. Federal law is not fundamentally opposed to the formation of medical practices as corporate bodies (public companies, limited companies, cooperatives), but the legislation of certain cantons make this very difficult since they have high standards when it comes to licensing corporate bodies as medical practices.

586. The KVG also expressly provides for the medical licensing of corporate bodies in which a group of doctors is employed (Article 36a, KVG).

§2. Healthcare Centres

587. As with group practices, private outpatient healthcare centres have also been on the increase in recent years. They are still not very numerous and are primarily concentrated in urban areas, but they fulfil an obvious demand for quick outpatient treatment outside the traditional hospital structure. Furthermore, the outpatient activities of hospitals have greatly increased over the last few years, which is partially owing to new methods of treatment. But the pressure within hospitals to cut costs, which has led to a reduction of hospital beds, has also played a role.

§3. PROFESSIONAL DUTIES TOWARDS COLLEAGUES

588. Professional law in the wider sense also regulates the physician's relationship to his or her professional colleagues. Collegiality among doctors is therefore less a legal obligation than it is an imperative of polite and tactful behaviour. This means that mutual collegial duties are primarily regulated in private professional law and not in public occupational law. In most cases, there is no public interest at stake in abidance or non-abidance of the relevant professional rules.

589. Professional law obliges doctors to maintain collegial relations with one another. These relations are defined by honesty and politeness (Article 23, paragraph 1, StaO FMH). In relation to third parties, doctors must remain factual and objective in any remarks on the medical approaches and treatments of colleagues. This imperative of objectivity also holds for cooperative work between doctors and it must always be channelled toward the careful and conscientious practice of one's profession so as to ensure the patient's well-being. The professional rules concretely articulate how doctors should work together and how patients should be hospitalized, and it is regarded as uncooperative to coax a patient away from a colleague who is treating the patient. It is a professional obligation to support younger colleagues. Whenever possible, disputes should be amicably resolved.

590. Only in qualified cases do the mentioned professional obligations contravene public occupational law – e.g., when a doctor, in dealings with colleagues, uses means that are prohibited by law. Limits are set here by the protection offered personal rights under both private and penal law. Levelling unjust allegations against colleagues is incompatible with the general duty of diligent and conscientious practice of one's profession. The doctor who casts slurs on colleagues and makes them look ridiculous behaves in a manner that earns neither trust nor respect.

591. In addition, from the perspective of both occupational and professional law, a doctor's conduct towards his or her colleagues can be relevant in the three scenarios discussed in the following three paragraphs.

592. Collegiality or collegial obligations may not be used as a pretext to cover up a colleague's faulty treatment of a patient, particularly when it goes against the patient's own best interest. The patient's well-being is the top priority. The standing of the medical profession is not preserved by *keeping* a colleague's mistakes *secret* but by *full disclosure*. The obligation to behave in a collegial fashion is not a prohibition of criticism but rather an obligation to be factual and objective – precisely in those circumstances when it is a professional imperative that the actions of a colleague be criticized with a view to protecting the interests of the patient.

593. Professional confidentiality is to be preserved vis-à-vis third parties who are themselves obligated to maintain confidentiality. Doctors are thus obliged to preserve patient confidentiality vis-à-vis colleagues even if there exists a scientific interest in knowing a (non-anonymized) clinical history. A patient's tacit consent to the disclosure of confidential information can be assumed, as a rule, if it is necessary to successful fulfilment of one's mandate. In such cases, the attending physician may share his or her knowledge with the specialists he or she has brought in on the case with the patient's approval.

594. Physicians must treat and advise their patients impartially and objectively according to professional criteria. All of a physician's actions should aim at the patient's well-being. Any financial advantages accruing to the doctor that (might) oppose the patient's best interest are inadmissible; the physician's own financial interests must take a backseat. For instance, a doctor may not refer patients to other doctors and hospitals or have patients examined and treated by certain entities against the promise of financial reward.

Chapter 2. Relationship with Other Healthcare Providers

§1. Pharmacists

595. In Switzerland, primary healthcare is mainly provided by doctors in private practice and by hospitals. In contrast to other countries, it is not the local pharmacies that ensure primary healthcare.

596. The relationship between doctors and pharmacists is structured accordingly. Pharmacists may only sell without a prescription those medicines that do not require such according to stipulations set down in the legislation concerning medicines. If a certain medicine requires a prescription, it is necessary that this comes from a qualified doctor. Pharmacists, who are equally well trained, may not dispense medicines that require a prescription solely on their own authority. With the revision of the HMG (*Heilmittelgesetz*), which was adopted in March 2016, the pharmacists get the permission to sell some specifically marked medicines without a prescription of a doctor, if they document those disposals.

597. It is currently a point of issue whether doctors should continue to be allowed to sell medicines themselves or whether they should limit themselves to prescribing medicines that are then sold to patients by pharmacists. In the canton of Zurich, there have already been several referendums on this question, and most have repeatedly voted to allow for the possibility of doctors' dispensing medicines.

598. At the Federal level, within the framework of health insurance legislation, there is currently a discussion as to whether physicians should be fundamentally constrained in their dispensing of medicines. But no decision is in the offing.

§2. Midwives

599. As part of the health insurance programme, midwives are licensed to work as self-employed healthcare providers; that is, there is coverage for outpatient midwife services for both women who are expecting and those in childbed.

600. Occasionally, self-employed gynaecologists work together with self-employed midwives. And even if it is not a terribly widespread phenomenon, midwives can also be employed in gynaecological practices.

§3. Paramedical Professionals

601. Health insurance also covers the various paramedical professions (physiotherapy, ergotherapy, nutrition counselling, etc.), regardless of whether the practitioners are self-employed or their work is delegated by a physician.

602. Frequently such healthcare providers are directly employed by a medical practice: A physician delegates his or her services, which are performed in the practice itself.

Chapter 3. Relationship with Healthcare Institutions

§1. Hospitals

603. There are various ways in which physicians can work together with hospitals: as assistant staff doctors, senior or chief physicians, and as self-employed inpatient doctors who only occasionally utilize the hospital infrastructure to carry out operations and perform other tasks.

604. Until just a few years ago, the positions for doctors in hospitals were predominantly short-term arrangements; that is to say, within the framework of their advanced training, they occupied various posts as assistant doctors so that they might then go on to establish practices of their own or continue specialist training in the position of senior physician. Only supervisory senior physicians and chief physicians had the prospect of remaining in their hospital posts for a longer period of time.

605. But in the last few years, hospital conditions have changed. Due to the aforementioned licensing moratorium for physicians in private practice, young doctors have increasingly been forced to remain on hospital staffs for longer periods. Therefore, alongside the traditional hierarchy of doctors in hospitals, there also emerged the post of hospital physician, who remained employed for a long time as an assistant doctor despite having completed his or her advanced training. In this way, the employment model in Swiss hospitals has more closely approximated conditions in various of its neighbouring European States, where the position of hospital doctor is regularly of indefinite duration.

§2. Health Insurance

I. Doctors as Healthcare Providers in the Health Insurance Programme

606. The relationship to the health insurance programme plays an important role for self-employed doctors in Switzerland since large portions of their services are paid for by health insurers. It is therefore of paramount importance that they be recognized by the health insurers as healthcare providers. A variety of conditions must be fulfilled for this to be the case. On the one hand the doctor must be licensed to practice as a self-employed physician, and on the other hand, the KVG demands that the doctor fulfil certain prerequisites so that his or her activities will be covered by compulsory health insurance. According to Article 34 of the Medical Professions Law, in order to be licensed to practise an academic medical profession in a self-employed capacity, one requires authorization from that canton where the medical profession is to be practised. Prerequisites for this authorization, according to Article 36 of the Medical Professions Law, are that the applicant holds an appropriate degree, is trustworthy, and offers physical and psychological guarantees that he or she will be able to faultlessly perform his or her duties. Additionally, the doctor must possess either a Swiss postgraduate degree or a foreign degree that is recognized as comparable. In order to have a medical practice covered by health insurance, Article 36 of the KVG requires that a doctor hold the Swiss degree and that he or she possess a postgraduate degree that is recognized by the Federal Council. There is no formal process for licensing. All doctors who fulfil the prerequisites for self-employed medical practice simultaneously fulfil those for having their medical practice covered by compulsory health insurance. Consequently, every doctor who receives cantonal licensing to practise must simultaneously be recognized by the health insurers as a healthcare provider (the health insurers' obligation to contract).

607. It should be noted that doctors are not required to charge their services to the compulsory health insurance. If a healthcare provider is not inclined to render any services in line with the KVG, he or she can decide to work outside the system, but must report this to a centre designated by the cantonal government (Article 44 KVG). Such action has a universal effect – i.e., it cannot be declared only in relation to certain services, health insurers, or patients.

II. Repeal of the Obligation to Contract

608. Due to steadily rising costs in healthcare, greater restrictions were placed on the authorization to charge services to the compulsory health insurance in 2002, and a cap was imposed on the number of healthcare providers per canton. But according to Article 55a of the KVG, this measure is only possible for a limited period of time. Article 55a of the KVG will only be in force until 30 June 2019. For the future, therefore, other possibilities will have to be sought in order to curb and reduce costs. One proposal is that freedom of contract should be introduced into the relationship between insurer and healthcare provider, which means that the obligation to contract should be repealed and the health insurer should be allowed to choose which healthcare provider he or she would like to work with.

609. This means that physicians who are healthcare providers would no longer have any automatic claim to being licensed to charge services to the compulsory health insurance – even if they fulfil the legal requirements regarding entry-level and postgraduate education as well as the requirements with respect to quality and cost effectiveness. The idea behind this is that increased competition among healthcare providers will lower costs. In order to ensure healthcare, the cantons would be permitted to stipulate how many healthcare providers the insurers could conclude contracts with.

III. Insured Services

610. The prerequisite for health insurers to assume the costs of a physician's services is that they serve the diagnosis or treatment of an ailment and its consequences. Furthermore, these services must be effective, appropriate, and economical. Applicable here is the legal supposition that a doctor's services have fulfilled the prerequisites for an assumption of costs on the part of the compulsory health insurance. But the lists in the appendix of the Health Insurance Service Ordinance (KLV) must also be taken into account. These include not only new or contested services whose costs are wholly or partially assumed, but also those services whose costs are not covered or are covered only in a provisional fashion if certain conditions are met.

611. In principle, a physician's services should be personally rendered. However, health insurers will also assume the cost of those services that the doctor delegates to auxiliary staff as long as these services are performed under the direct supervision of the physician. These auxiliary staff can include physiotherapists, ergotherapists, qualified care attendants, speech therapists, and nutritionists.

IV. Regulations on Fees

612. In terms of those services whose costs are assumed by the compulsory health insurance, doctors cannot themselves set prices; rather, they bill for their services within the framework of the TARMED ('*tarif médical*') agreement. The basic TARMED agreement for outpatient services in medical practices was concluded between the *santésuisse* (the branch association of Swiss Health Insurers) and the FMH (Alliance of Swiss Doctors). This agreement is an attempt to create a price structure. A physician's services are converted into so-called tax points ('*Taxpunkte*'). The value of the individual tax point can vary depending on region.

Selected Bibliography

Aebi-Müller, Regina & Fellmann, Walter & Gächter, Thomas & Rütsche, Bernhard & Tag, Brigitte, Arztrecht, Berne, 2016.

Ayer, Ariane, et al. (eds). *Medizinalberufegesetz (MedBG), Kommentar*. Basel, 2009.

Bertrand, Dominique, et al. (eds). *Médecin et droit médical: présentation et résolution de situations médico-légales*. 3rd ed. Chêne-Bourg, 2009.

Büchler, Andrea & Michel, Margot. *Medizin – Mensch – Recht. Eine Einführung in das Medizinrecht der Schweiz*. Zurich, 2014.

Dörr, BiankaSofie & Michel, Margot (eds). *Biomedizinrecht. Herausforderungen – Entwicklungen – Perspektiven*. St Gallen/Zurich, 2007.

Eichenberger, Thomas & Marti, Mario. *Recht für Ärzte – Einführung in die Grundlagen. Gesundheitsrecht für Ärzte und Juristen*. Berne, 2004.

Elger Bernice S., Biller-Andorno, Nikola & Rütsche, Bernhard (eds). *Ethik und Recht in Medizin und Biowissenschaften*. Berlin, 2014.

Gächter, Thomas & Rütsche, Bernhard. *Gesundheitsrecht*. 3rd ed. Basel, 2013.

Kocher, Gerhard & Oggier, Willy (eds). *Gesundheitswesen Schweiz, 2010–2012, Eine aktuelle Übersicht*. 4th ed. Berne, 2010.

Kuhn, Moritz & Poledna, Tomas (eds). *Arztrecht in der Praxis*. Zurich/Basel/Geneva, 2007.

Landolt, Hardy. *Öffentliches Gesundheitsrecht, Public Health Law*. Zurich/St Gallen, 2009.

Lendfers, Miriam & Kieser, Ueli. *Gesundheitsrecht in a nutshell*. Zürich/St Gallen, 2013.

Manaï, Dominique. *Droit du patient et biomédecine*. 3rd ed. Berne, 2013.

Meyer, Ulrich (ed.). 'Soziale Sicherheit', vol. XIV. In *Schweizerisches Bundesverwaltungsrecht*. Edited by Heinrich Koller et al., 3rd ed. Basel, 2015.

Poledna, Tomas & Berger, Brigitte. *Öffentliches Gesundheitsrecht*. Berne, 2002.

Poledna, Tomas & Kieser, Ueli (eds). 'Gesundheitsrecht', vol. VIII. In *Schweizerisches Bundesverwaltungsrecht*. Edited by Heinrich Koller et al. Basel/Geneva/Munich, 2005.

Schaffhauser, René, Kieser, Ueli & Poledna, Tomas (eds). *Das neue Medizinalberufegesetz (MedBG)*. St Gallen, 2008.

Selected Bibliography

Index

The numbers here refer to paragraph numbers.

Index

Index

Index

www.ingramcontent.com/pod-product-compliance
Lightning Source LLC
Chambersburg PA
CBHW071340230926
51846CB00002B/400
9789041182654